HEROES BEHIND THE MASK

America's Greatest Catchers

HEROES
BEHIND THE MASK

America's Greatest Catchers

by

Milton J. Shapiro

Illustrated with photographs

JULIAN MESSNER  NEW YORK

Published simultaneously in the United States and Canada by
Julian Messner, a division of Simon & Schuster, Inc.,
1 West 39 Street, New York, N.Y. 10018. All rights reserved.

Second Printing, 1969

Photo credits United Press International
Pages 78, 118, 165 and 175.

Printed in the United States of America
Library of Congress Catalog Card No. 68-25106

To Herb Goren, Jack Orr, Berry Stainback and Wayne Hall, and to the many others who helped with the preparation and the consensus for this book.

Contents

Yogi Berra

1

THE city of St. Louis is not a summer resort. You can fry eggs on the sidewalk in July, and by August the air has the consistency of vaporized dishwater. The baseball parks are turned into huge ovens, baking the soil of the diamonds into hard clay. Only the followers and players of baseball are mad enough to go out in the noonday sun.

In the summer of 1940, Lawrence Peter Berra—better known as Yogi to his friends—was both follower and player. As others withered, he blossomed under the summer sun, devouring the sports pages for news of his beloved St. Louis Cardinals, scampering around the sandlot diamonds playing for the Stockham Post of the American Legion. Short, stocky, ungainly and unhandsome, with long arms and no neck, he was the butt of much good-humored joking from his friends. But what he could do with a baseball bat was no laughing matter—at least to the opposing pitcher.

"That kid can really hit," said Leo Browne, who

11

managed the Stockham team. "Tremendous power for a fifteen-year-old. And he doesn't care where you pitch it, he murders the ball."

Yogi wasn't much of a glove man, and Browne rotated him between catching and the outfield. When he was in the outfield his friend Joe Garagiola did the catching. When he caught, often Garagiola would pitch.

The two boys were local heroes to the youngsters of the neighborhood, playing as they did with Stockham. Browne, a former minor league umpire, put together excellent teams. But to their fathers, Yogi and Joe were terrible problems. Pietro Berra and Giovanni Garagiola had left Italy together many years before and settled on The Hill, the Little Italy section of St. Louis. There they worked hard in the local brickyard and began raising a family in the traditions they had brought with them from Italy.

Playing baseball was not one of those traditions. A friendly game of *bocce* on a Sunday afternoon with a few *paisani*—a few countrymen—was all right. But this baseball! That's all the boys talked about, and as soon as the good weather came, they were always running off somewhere to play. They even talked about playing someday for money, for a living! Often at night the two old friends would get together and laugh about their sons' fanatical interest in baseball, but sometimes they were seriously annoyed.

Pietro Berra was particularly bothered. He had been forced to squelch the ambitions of his three older sons, who had wanted to become baseball players. Now it was his baby, Laudi—or Larry, or worse yet, Yogi, as they called him here—who wanted to be a baseball player. Such nonsense!

True, if a boy wants to work, let him work, Pietro Berra believed. When Laudi came to him last year and said he wanted to quit school and go to work, he let him go, did he not? But what did the boy do? Get a steady job? Learn a trade? No! He went from job to job, a week here, a month there, and when the weather became warm and the boys started playing baseball—off the job he went so he would have more time to play.

Thinking these things, Pietro Berra would shake his head and sigh, wondering what would become of his boy.

He wondered thus through Yogi's early teens, as the youngster went from factory hand to helper on a soft-drink truck to busboy to apprentice brickyard worker to —well, to a dozen different jobs. Through them all he threaded a path of baseball. Few people took his diamond aspirations seriously. In fact, you could have counted those few on the fingers of one hand—and have two fingers left over. Aside from Yogi himself, only his friend Gara-giola and Leo Browne, his manager, had much faith in his baseball future.

In the summer of 1942, when Yogi was seventeen, Browne arranged a tryout for him and Garagiola with the Cardinals. Among the judges that day at Sportsman's Park was Branch Rickey, owner of the Cardinals at the time. Both boys were trying out as catchers. Garagiola went first, batting, catching one of the Cardinals' batting practice pitchers, pouncing on bunts and throwing to first, second and third.

Then came Yogi's turn. Nervously he took his place behind the plate. He knew he could hit and could catch, but he had little confidence in his throwing arm. It was strong but erratic. A few moments later, when he was tested, his nervousness accentuated his lack of accuracy. Repeatedly he threw wildly to the bases.

At the plate later he redeemed himself in part by clouting the ball solidly. Still, when he and Garagiola dressed later and waited to see Rickey in the clubhouse offices, he felt he had lost his chance.

Again Garagiola went first. In short order he was out

again, a grin splitting his face. "I made it, Yogi!" he exclaimed. "They're gonna send me to Springfield. And they gave me a five-hundred-dollar bonus!"

Yogi shook his friend's hand warmly and patted him on the back. Then he, too, went in to see Branch Rickey.

The Cardinals' boss gazed kindly at the youngster from beneath his great shaggy eyebrows. A blue cloud of smoke rose upward from a cigar held clenched between his teeth.

Rickey took out the cigar and spoke. "You have a lot of spirit, my boy," he said. "And that's half the battle. But you're too small, and you're too wild. Next year, maybe . . ." He let his voice trail off.

But Yogi refused to be dismissed so easily. He pleaded for a chance. He would play anywhere. He was actually to the point of winning his argument, but when the subject of money arose, he insisted on the same five-hundred-dollar bonus given to his friend Garagiola.

This was too much for Rickey. He wasn't impressed with this funny-looking little youngster in the first place. And here the boy was, demanding a bonus! He promptly closed the interview and almost threw Yogi out of his office.

The Cardinals came that close to owning Berra. It was one of the few mistakes in human judgment ever made by the great Mahatma Rickey.

Yogi was bitterly disappointed. More than that, he even felt shame. They always laughed at him on The Hill because of his funny appearance. The boys had even tagged him Yogi because he looked like some yogi from India in a movie they had all seen. Now they would laugh all the more because Garagiola had made it and he hadn't.

Leo Browne was also disappointed, but he was not discouraged. He felt that Yogi had the raw power and the will to make a professional ballplayer. Accordingly, he

14

soothed the boy's wounded pride and promised he would get him another tryout.

Browne's reputation among the baseball scouts was a good one. He wasn't constantly clamoring about a "new Babe Ruth" he had discovered. However, he had through the years sent along a number of players who had at least made the major leagues, though none had become stars. When he recommended a youngster, therefore, a scout went around for a look.

It came about then, that scout Johnny Schulte of the Yankees was in St. Louis. Browne collared him and talked him into viewing one of the Stockham games. "I got a catcher can hit the ball a mile," he said.

"Can he catch?" asked Schulte.

"You can teach him how to catch," replied Browne. "As a hitter he's a natural. No style, but what power!"

Schulte went along to the game. He saw exactly what Browne had described. As a receiver the youngster was just adequate. At the plate it was a different story. Yogi blasted the ball all over the park, hitting high outside pitches, low inside pitches—anything anywhere near the plate.

"He can hit all right," said the Yankee scout. "But what kind of pitches is he swinging at?"

"He's a natural bad-ball hitter," Browne said. "Lots of sluggers are. Remember Joe Medwick?" he asked, reminding Schulte about the Cardinals' great Gas House Gang star.

Schulte nodded. "Okay, I'll sign the kid."

There were two obstacles to overcome, however. First, when they talked after the game, Yogi was not so overwhelmed at his good fortune that he forgot to ask for his five-hundred-dollar bonus. To hold his head up among the kids in the neighborhood, he had to get the same as Garagiola.

That part was easy. Schulte agreed. The second obstacle was Pietro Berra. He was still dead set against Yogi's baseball ambitions, still regarded them as boyish foolishness that had nothing to do with reality. Schulte couldn't help there. This obstacle Berra would have to overcome himself.

Yogi enlisted the aid of his brothers. Together they confronted their father that evening, telling him of the offer to join the Yankees' farm system, and about the bonus.

Mr. Berra was unimpressed.

The boys drew out all the arguments they could think of. Baseball was indeed a game for good Italian boys, they said. Especially with the Yankees. Look at Rizzuto, and DiMaggio, and Lazzeri. And, for that matter, hadn't his old friend Giovanni allowed his boy Joey to play baseball? Were the Garagiolas to be allowed honors denied the Berras?

What went on in Pietro Berra's mind during this harangue can only be guessed. But one suspects the argument of family pride carried more weight than the mention of Italian-sounding names. What did they mean to him? Who was this Rizzuto and this DiMaggio? Their fathers probably didn't even come from the same province as he did.

But . . . if Giovanni's son could play baseball, then Pietro's son could play baseball, too.

"Okay, okay," he said at last. "Go. Go become a-a whatyoucallit. A Yankee!"

Yogi was sent to Norfolk, Virginia, in the spring of 1943. This was the Class B Piedmont League, a comparatively ambitious beginning for a boy just out of American Legion ball. The country was at war, however, and baseball talent was short. Not quite eighteen when he went to Norfolk, Yogi was too young to be drafted.

He had a decent year as a catcher in Norfolk, batting .253, with 7 homers and 56 runs batted in, playing in 111 games.

The Yankees were impressed enough to promote him to Kansas City for 1944, a Triple A farm. Like many a patriotic youngster, however, Yogi didn't wait around for the war to catch up with him—he went out after it. He joined the Navy instead of Kansas City, reporting soon after the 1943 season had ended.

After training, Yogi reported for sea duty, and saw action aboard a ship giving covering fire during the Allied invasion of Normandy in June of 1944. When his sea tour was finished the Navy sent him back to New London, Connecticut. There, assigned to Welfare and Recreation, he resumed his baseball activities on the base's team.

He was on his terminal leave in the spring of 1946— still in uniform but waiting to be discharged—when typical backstage maneuvering had a profound effect on his baseball career. Somebody had tipped off Mel Ott, manager of the Giants, that the Yankees had a hot catching prospect they were hiding. The youngster, Berra, was just getting out of the Navy.

Ott went around to see Larry McPhail, president of the Yankees, and offered fifty thousand dollars for Berra. McPhail had never even heard of Yogi Berra. However, he was an astute enough businessman to realize that if the Giants were offering fifty thousand for a kid on one of his farm teams, it wouldn't do to sell him without further investigation. He turned down the offer, then sent for Yogi's records and Yogi himself.

Neither impressed McPhail. True enough, neither was much to look at. McPhail began to wonder whether or not he had blundered, refusing fifty thousand dollars for such an unlikely-looking prospect. Still, Ott was no fool. Maybe, thought McPhail, Ott knew something he didn't know.

The question was now, where to play Yogi for 1946. McPhail decided on Newark. It was a bold move; Newark, in the International League, was just one step below the Yankees. The way McPhail figured it, however, if the kid really had anything on the ball, he would make it in Newark. If he hadn't the stuff, might as well find out now and peddle him to some other team. Maybe to Ott, for that fifty thousand.

Yogi was astounded at his rapid and unexpected rise. Two years in the Navy and the whine of bullets around his ears had considerably matured him, however. Rather than being frightened, worried that he might be out of his depth, he looked forward to the challenge. Eagerly he changed his Navy uniform for that of the Newark Bears.

Manager George Selkirk, a former Yankee outfielder, was not enchanted to get him. He had expected a pitcher, and instead received an inexperienced catcher-outfielder who looked more like a—well, who looked like anything but a ballplayer.

Yogi didn't break into the Newark lineup immediately. Selkirk kept him on the bench for a while, unwilling to start him. Finally, impressed with the way Berra was splattering the ball around in batting practice day after day, the Bears' manager gave him his chance. Yogi came through at once, belting the high-class International League pitching as though it were sandlot stuff. Behind the plate he would give Selkirk fits sometimes, particularly when he had to throw, but what he did with his bat more than made up for any slight deficiency defensively.

Playing 77 games for Newark, he hit .312 with 15 homers and 59 runs batted in, an extraordinary half-season's work.

There was a week left to play in the major league season. Customarily, the big league teams bring up a few

18

promising youngsters in the final week, giving them a feel of major league atmosphere. If the team is not involved in a tight pennant race, the newcomers get to play. The Yankees were out of contention at the closing moments of the 1946 season, in third place. Therefore, when they called up Yogi, Bobby Brown and Frank Colman in that final week, they immediately thrust them into the lineup.

It all happened so quickly Yogi didn't have time to be awed by the presence of such storied Yankee heroes as Joe DiMaggio, Tommy Henrich, Vic Raschi, Spud Chandler and Phil Rizzuto. He just came in swinging. In his seven games with the Yankees he hit two homers and batted .364, with eight hits and four runs batted in.

Yankee president McPhail, who had been keeping a special eye on Berra ever since the offer by Mel Ott, watched those last seven games of the 1946 season. When it was all over he said to one of his aides, "Imagine that horse thief Ott, only offering fifty thousand for Berra!"

Baseball writers are forever searching for "characters." They enliven their existence, enrich their copy, add spice to their often humdrum daily reportage. On their part, most ball clubs do not discourage the search, and often lend a helping hand in the cultivation of such colorful players, knowing full well the dollar value of the ensuing publicity.

The New York Mets are outstanding examples. No team in baseball history ever made such a virtue of incompetence. Shrewdly, they became a collection of colorful characters instead of merely third-rate ballplayers; the fans loved them and crowded through the gates.

Traditionally, the Yankees abstained from such promotions. Even in the years when they had Babe Ruth and Leo Durocher and were managed by Miller Huggins they remained aloof from the kind of publicity grabbed by the St. Louis "Gas House Gang" and the "Bums," as the Brooklyn Dodgers were affectionately called. When New York City had three teams the Yankee pinstripes were considered aptly symbolic of the club's successful, conservative image, as opposed to the daffy doings of those all-time arch rivals of baseball, the Giants and the Dodgers.

When Lawrence Peter Berra arrived on the scene in spring training of 1947, therefore, with a nickname of Yogi and rather nonconventional physical features, the writers loved him at first sight. In addition, because of his amiable nature and intense desire to be accepted, he was easy to interview, and he readily accepted himself as the butt of jokes.

Sometimes the writers and his own teammates went too far, though unintentionally. They made cruel sport of his looks and his lack of education, his penchant for reading comic books and the things he said. Often enough, in his unsophisticated manner, he did say funny things, but the stories that quickly sprang up about him were as likely to be apocryphal as not. The thing was, with Yogi, all the stories were so typical they *could* have been true. After a while, nobody could tell the truth from legend, even Yogi himself.

In spring training of 1947, for example, it was quickly noted that he swung at anything he could reach. Manager Bucky Harris repeatedly pleaded with him to restrict his swings to balls somewhere at least around the strike zone. "Think when you're up there, Yogi. Think!" Harris said.

To which Yogi irritatedly muttered to another player, "How can I think and hit the ball at the same time!"

The fact that this story is attributed to both Bucky Harris and Casey Stengel, who became manager in 1949, is beside the point.

So are the origins of many other Yogi-isms. As a marvelous piece of irony, many of the Yogi Berra stories are attributed to his old friend, Joe Garagiola, for their roles reversed in later years. Garagiola, after an average career as a catcher, became an outstanding baseball humorist and radio-TV commentator, while Yogi, the clown of the pair in their youth, went on to become one of the all-time great catchers.

According to Garagiola, he was with Yogi when Berra was asked what he thought about Little League Baseball.

"I think it's good," Yogi said, "because it keeps the kids out of the house."

Tommy Henrich, a former Yankee outfield great, has his favorite Berra story, too.

One day Yogi was behind the plate when Jimmy Piersall of the Red Sox came up to hit. Piersall, subject of Al Hirshberg's book, *Fear Strikes Out,* had just returned to baseball after a stay in a mental institution. The two Boston hitters previous to Piersall had been knocked down by the Yankee pitcher. As he dug in, Jimmy said to Berra, "If this guy throws at me I'll wrap this bat around your neck. I can get away with it. I can plead temporary insanity."

Replied Yogi, "Look, boy, on this club we don't knock down no two-fifty hitters."

Until Stengel came along in 1949, Berra was the Yankees' one flash of color on an otherwise drab canvas. Often accused of being coldly efficient, winning World Championships with dispassionate ease, the Yankees were glad to have Yogi aboard.

True enough, however, he did give them bad moments. His fielding was not major league. Harris tried him in right field as well as behind the plate; in neither position did he do well. In the outfield he lacked confidence in judgment on fly balls, and his throwing arm was strong but erratic. He did better behind the plate, but here, too, his throwing arm failed him.

Harris favored Yogi as a catcher. "I don't think he'll ever have the speed and the grace to make an outfielder," the manager confided to the Yankee brass. "But we'll make a catcher out of him yet, if it kills us!"

One play at home plate on June 15 added to the manager's conviction that Yogi had the makings of a great catcher. It happened at the Stadium against the St. Louis Browns. The Brownies pulled a squeeze play. With catlike swiftness Yogi jumped on the bunt, lunged to his right, tagging out the batter, then spun and dived to his left, tagging out the runner sliding home from third. An unassisted double play!

Afterward, in the clubhouse, as he was being kidded about his rare feat, Yogi said, "All I did was grab the ball and tag everybody in sight."

"Including the umpire," added one sportswriter.

"Yeah," agreed Berra, "including the ump." Giving birth to another Yogi-ism.

Still another legend was added toward the latter part of his rookie season. When the team arrived in St. Louis for a series with the Browns, his old friends from The Hill gave him a testimonial night at Sportsman's Park. As he stood at home plate that night, surrounded by gifts, he was more nervous than he had been on his first at-bat in professional ball.

Knees quaking and voice quivering, he grasped the microphone to give his brief speech. He gulped hard and said: "I want to thank everyone who made this night necessary."

There was a moment of stunned silence from the crowd, then a roar of laughter from the huge stadium. As he went smiling back to the dugout, he was trying to figure out the reason for the laughter, until a teammate told him. "Hey, Yogi, you were supposed to say, 'who made this night *possible.*'"

As usual, however, the noise he was making with his bat all season served to drown out the laughter. Because of his unorthodox batting style and habit of swinging at bad pitches, everybody waited for the day when the shrewd major league pitchers would begin to tie him up in knots. They waited in vain. Yogi hit everybody and anything they threw at him.

A serious strep-throat infection curtailed his playing during the last month of his first season, and weakened his power. When the 1947 season ended, with an easy Yankee pennant, Yogi had a .280 average with 11 homers and 54 runs batted in, playing 83 games.

The World Series was a near disaster for him. Playing in a World Series is always tough for a rookie, with the tense atmosphere of high drama and the World Championship at stake. For Yogi, picked as opening game catcher, there was an extra burden. The National League champions were the Dodgers, a running team, led by Jackie Robinson. A rookie himself and the first Negro in organized baseball, Robinson had driven National League pitchers crazy with his base running heroics. He was fast, daring and smart, without question the best base runner in the major leagues.

Before the first game of the World Series was under way everybody in the ball park—indeed in all baseball— knew what to expect. Robinson would try to steal everything but Yogi Berra's shoes.

Unhappily for Yogi, that's just about the way it happened. To Berra's credit it must be said that Robinson did it to the best and most experienced catchers in the National League, and led the league in stolen bases that year.

Benched in the third game, relegated to right field for half of the sixth game, he got little joy out of the

1947 Series, though the Yankees won in seven games. A pinch-hit homer in the third game was his only contribution of note.

He felt alone in the midst of the Yankee celebration following the final game. He even wondered about his future. Would the Yankees try to trade him, send him back to the minors for more experience?

He was still plunged in gloom and worry when manager Harris came over to him and put his arm around him. "Boys," Harris announced to the newsmen, "meet my number-one catcher for next season."

Berra wasn't the only man surprised by the announcement. Many of the sportswriters and Yankee players were equally amazed. Not that any of them had doubts about Yogi's future worth. There was little question of his potential. Most had figured, however, that he was a year or two away from a regular berth as Yankee receiver.

Bucky Harris had no such reservations. Or, if he had, he shelved them in light of the necessities of the moment. The Yankees needed hitting. They could use a good-hitting catcher. Aside from Berra, their present receivers were Aaron Robinson and Sherman Lollar. Both were adequate defense men, but no more than that. Neither man could hit. To Harris, this meant Berra went to the head of the catching department. His philosophy was, you could teach a good hitter to catch, but not vice versa.

There were times during the 1948 season when Harris wondered whether that philosophy wasn't more wishful thinking than sound baseball theory. Occasionally Yogi would come up with the big play, and enemy runners didn't always feel free to steal a base. For the most part he was proving a handicap behind the plate, however. It was noticeable less in his throwing and fielding than in his handling of pitchers. The veterans had little confidence in him, in his calling of pitches. A few, in

24

fact, complained privately that with a man on first he called too many fast balls, trying for an extra break against a possible steal.

Harris and the Yankee coaches worked with him daily. Certainly he was improving, absorbing information. But handling of pitchers requires their confidence, which in turn means the catcher has to have an excellent "book" on the hitters. This takes time to accumulate.

As the 1948 season wore on, Harris was running out of time. The team was not winning. He knew Yogi was somewhat of a handicap behind the plate, and in fact was hurting himself there as well at the moment, fretting and worrying and thus affecting his hitting.

In August he shifted Yogi to right field, brought right-fielder Tommy Henrich in to play first in place of poor-hitting George McQuinn, and brought Gus Niarhos in to catch. The move did spark the Yankees for a few weeks. Relieved of mounting pressures, Yogi, too, rebounded. He played right field decently, if not brilliantly, and his bat once again boomed all over the circuit.

It was not the Yankees' year, no matter what they tried. The Indians won the pennant, with the Yankees third. Yogi hit a solid .305, with 14 homers and 98 runs batted in. There could be no complaints about his hitting.

It might be said, in hindsight, that the Yankees' failure in 1948 was a key factor in the success of Yogi Berra. Failure meant that Bucky Harris was fired. Casey Stengel was hired as the new Yankee manager. Casey promptly hired Bill Dickey as a Yankee coach, which made all the difference in the world to Berra's future as a catcher.

Dickey was the best catcher the Yankees ever had, and without question one of the all-time greats of baseball history. If anybody could make a catcher out of Berra, it would be this soft-spoken master of the trade.

At once Dickey realized that Berra's immediate problems were desire and confidence. With the latter, he was sure, would come desire. He felt that two tough years behind the plate had broken Yogi's confidence in himself as a catcher, and that he therefore showed little enthusiasm for the position.

In spring training of 1949 Dickey took him in hand. He taught him the fundamentals of catching, something nobody had ever done before. Yogi, in effect, had been little more than a sandlot catcher getting by on sheer instinct and strength. Dickey showed him how to catch, how to throw, how to go after foul balls, how to play bunts. He showed Yogi that he had been squatting too far back of the hitter, losing important split seconds in receiving the pitch and getting it away when a steal was on.

"You've been rushing the throws and pushing," Dickey explained patiently, "because you're afraid the ball won't get to second in time. But it doesn't do any good to get the ball there in a hurry if it goes over the infielder's head or skips by him. Once you realize you have time enough, you'll improve your accuracy. Remember that most steals are made against the pitcher, not the catcher, and there are just some that *no* catcher can stop."

Slowly, but with definite forward motion, Dickey got through to him. He told Yogi that he, too, had suffered setbacks in the beginning. But if he had the desire to learn, the *will* to be the best, Yogi could become one of the best.

Dickey believed this, too. It was just not the coach speaking to the pupil. "He's got something, this kid," he said to Stengel one day. "He's been pushed around and he's down on himself. But he's quick, he's got the baseball instinct, and of course he can murder the ball. Once he gains confidence, once he proves to himself on the ball field that he's got the stuff, I predict he'll become one of the game's great catchers."

This seemed like a rash prediction based on the evidence. Stengel cocked his scrawny head and looked at Dickey with shrewd eyes. If Dickey said it, then there must be truth in it, Stengel figured. Berra was going to be his boy. He decided then and there to stick with him.

The change in Yogi did not come overnight, but it came quickly. As the 1949 season unfolded he improved day by day. Certainly he continued to make mistakes, but he was a solid receiver. Stengel's growing respect for him as a handler of pitchers grew, too. Soon the entire league was looking at Yogi and laughing differently at him now. He was still the butt of good-humored needling—he always would be—but there were a respect and an acceptance behind it now that had been lacking earlier.

How much he had improved that spring and early summer was reflected in his selection for the All-Star team along with Birdie Tebbets of the Red Sox.

He rolled along in high gear through July and into August, hitting close to three hundred and leading the team in runs batted in. Then, on August 7, the day after he had beaten the St. Louis Browns with a grand slam homer, his thumb was broken by a pitched ball. He was out of action for a full month, and when he returned, thumb still swollen and stiff, he could hardly grip the bat.

Now he was a different Yogi Berra. This time he was wanted in the lineup as a catcher, not a hitter. "He knows his stuff," Stengel told the sportswriters. "I depend on him to handle the pitchers."

Yogi helped guide the Yankees through a tough battle to another pennant and World Championship. The pitchers had confidence in him now, and rarely shook off his signs. Though his hitting fell away sharply

27

in final weeks because of the thumb injury, he finished the season with a .277 average, 91 runs batted in and 20 homers.

Everything jelled for him the following year. Full of good health, brimming with confidence, he became the best catcher in the league. Dickey and Stengel were amazed at his rapid development. "I tell you one thing," Dickey told the sportswriters. "Yogi gets out after a bunt faster than I ever did."

The Yankees were good in 1950. So were the Tigers. The two teams fought a tremendous battle all season long, each grabbing the league lead for a while, then losing it to the other. Pitching was the Yankees' big trouble. With Yogi leading the hitters, closely followed by DiMaggio and Phil Rizzuto, they were getting the runs. But they were giving up more. Finally, in a thrill-packed series with Detroit in mid-September, they took two out of three games, regained the lead, and held on to win the pennant.

Their momentum carried them right through a four-game sweep of the Phillies in the World Series, Yogi contributing a homer and a single in the final 5–2 victory.

Nobody questioned his place in the Yankee picture now. He had hit .322 for the season, with 27 homers and 124 runs batted in. He received substantial support for the Most Valuable Player Award, but lost out to teammate Phil Rizzuto, who also had completed one of the finest seasons in his distinguished career.

There was a new look about the Yankees in the spring of 1951, and it wasn't just their different training camp. They were in Phoenix, Arizona, trading places with the Giants that year, instead of Florida. These were Yankees of a new era. Gone were most of the prewar heroes. The immortal DiMaggio, plagued by terrible injuries, was in decline. This was to be his last season.

28

The new look was exemplified by such players as Whitey Ford, who had a spectacular rookie pitching season the year before, by the presence of Berra, Stengel, and two youngsters just up from the minor leagues—Gil McDougald and Mickey Mantle.

Starting his fifth full season as a Yankee, Yogi was in fact the dean of the new young Yankees, though he retained much of the simple ingenuousness he had when he first joined the club. He was still a favorite target of the bench jockeys, though more sensitive to remarks about his physical appearance now that he was a married man with a son.

He never angered, however. That spring, when Birdie Tebbets, a notorious bench jockey, yelled at him, "How's your wife like living in a tree, Yogi?" Berra growled at him and replied, "Aw, I don't hit with my face."

Again, his bat answered best. He finished spring training with a .397 batting average. Everybody predicted he was heading for his biggest year.

Yet, unaccountably, when the season began he fell into a slump. He couldn't get his average above .250. The rest of the team wasn't much better; some were worse. DiMaggio was hitting .273, Johnny Mize under .200, MVP Rizzuto barely above .200.

Casey Stengel called a special batting drill one day. When Yogi took his turn in the batting cage, Stengel watched him carefully as he took his first few swings. "You're swinging behind the pitch," Stengel said to him.

Berra nodded and went back to work.

The long drill helped. Slowly his average began to climb. Behind the plate there was no faulting him, though the wobbly Yankee pitching staff was giving him a hard time. There were longer games, extra-inning games, wild pitching, batter after batter going to 3–2 situations.

A scatter-armed Tommy Byrne had him jumping all around the plate to haul in his pitches. (Byrne's roommate on the road trips was another wild lefty named Bob Wiesler, who used to walk a dozen or so a game. "What I don't understand," said a sportswriter one day, "is those two guys in the same room. How does either of them have enough control to put the key in the lock?")

Yogi stayed in there, responding to the pressure, maneuvering the pitchers, coming through with key hits to win ball games. He went on a ten-game hitting streak, brought his average up to .309 in July. One day he beat Bobby Shants, the A's tough little lefty, with a homer and a double, the two-bagger coming in the ninth with two out and winning the game.

"I'm not swinging for the seats now," he confided to Rizzuto after the game. "I figure I been trying too hard to hit homers. Pressing. Now I'm just hitting with the pitch."

Rizzuto looked at him curiously. Everybody knew Yogi loved to murder the ball. "Who stuck that idea in your head?" he asked.

"Well," Yogi said, "I heard Casey talking to that kid —you know, Mantle."

"Yeah? What did he say?"

"Case told him he didn't have to kill the ball to drive it out of the park. Just hit easy and let his natural power do the work. Well, I figure I'm a pretty strong guy, and it should work for me, too."

Rizzuto laughed. "Well, whattaya know, an eavesdropper!"

Yogi smacked him with a wet towel. "Yeah, well with your average, maybe *you* oughtta drop a few eaves once in a while."

The American League pennant race was a particularly hot one that summer. The Red Sox were in front by a narrow margin, trailed by the Yankees, the White

Sox and the Indians, all clumped together in a menacing bunch.

Then the Indians took over first place. Even a no-hitter thrown at them by Allie Reynolds in July couldn't dislodge them. They clung to first place until late August, when they suddenly began to fall apart, and the Yankees took over.

The climax came in mid-September. The Indians arrived in New York and threw their two big pitchers at the Yankees. But with Berra leading them, the Bombers beat Bob Feller, 4–1, and Bob Lemon, 2–1. That finished the Indians.

On the next to last day of the season, Allie Reynolds was on his way to his second no-hitter. He had two out in the ninth against the Red Sox, but Ted Williams, one of the greatest hitters of all time, was at the plate.

Berra called for the fast ball. It was good for a strike.

Another fast ball. Strike two.

Instead of calling for the waste pitch—truly a waste since Williams' keen eye had the strike zone measured with the accuracy of a micrometer—Yogi called for another fast ball.

Williams swung, got the edge of his bat on it, lifting a high twisting foul back of the plate. Yogi went after it. The ball, with considerable back spin on it, came down erratically. Yogi lunged for it, got the ball in his mitt, but it spun off and popped to the ground.

The crowd groaned. Yogi got up off his knees slowly, sick to his stomach. He couldn't bear to look at Reynolds. The pitcher's no-hitter was hanging on a slender thread; to give Williams a second chance was inviting disaster.

Yogi shuffled out to the mound. "I'm sorry, Wahoo," he said, choking. "I'm sorry."

"Forget it," Reynolds said, smiling, "we'll get him."

Yogi went back and called for still another fast ball. Williams swung—and sent another foul skyrocketing behind the plate. This one, high and twisting, near the dugout, was even tougher than the first one.

As Berra dashed over, Reynolds stayed with him. Near the lip of the dugout Yogi camped under the ball, waiting for it to come down. "Easy, Yogi, plenty of room," Reynolds said calmly as Berra took another step nearer the dugout.

Finally the ball plunged into the mitt. Yogi clamped it in the pocket, turned and leaped upon Reynolds. A second no-hitter!

In the World Series against the Giants that followed, Yogi got six hits, for a .261 average, and scored four runs, as the Yankees won in six games.

He had good reason to be satisfied with the way his life was going that fall of 1951. He had moved away from St. Louis, bought a house in New Jersey, lived there comfortably with his wife and two children. He and Rizzuto, a neighbor, had business interests going together in nearby Newark. All was right with Yogi's world.

He was sitting in his spacious living room one evening that fall when the phone rang. His wife, Carmen, answered, called to him from the kitchen that it was for him. He picked up the extension. The call was from Joe Reichler, baseball editor of the Associated Press.

"Guess what, Yogi," Reichler said. "They've named you Most Valuable Player in the American League!"

Yogi couldn't believe it. When newsmen trooped around to his house later that evening to interview him, he expressed his wonder in frank terms. "I think they shoulda picked Reynolds," he told the reporters. "With seventeen wins, and the two no-hitters, I thought sure Wahoo would get it."

It did seem strange to some observers that Yogi should win the MVP award with a record substantially inferior to the one he compiled in 1950, when he failed to win. But the tradition of the MVP is to look beyond the statistics to the overall values, the intangibles, the immeasurable qualities in a player that made him the most valuable man on his own team that year.

Yogi stood up to that test. He was so often the man with the clutch hit, the tireless receiver, the clever handler of pitchers, the silent field general. He was the first catcher to win the MVP in the American League since Mickey Cochrane of Detroit won in 1934.

The Yankees rolled on, crushing everybody in their wake through 1952 and 1953, beating the Dodgers both years for the World Championship. In 1952 Yogi established a new American League record for home runs in a season by a catcher, hitting 30. The following year, hitting .296 with 27 homers, he came through with a sensational World Series performance. He hit .429, with nine hits in six games, including a triple and a homer.

A couple of fielding gems in the 1953 Series opener at Yankee Stadium, however, distinguished him even more than his powerful hitting. It happened this way:

The Yankees were leading, 5–4, going into the seventh, but the Dodgers were getting at Johnny Sain, who had relieved Reynolds. Roy Campanella started the trouble with a single. Gil Hodges singled him to second. Then Furillo singled Campanella home with the tying run, Hodges stopping at second.

Up to the plate came Billy Cox, with two hits already in the game. Dodger manager Charley Dressen surprised everybody by giving Cox the bunt sign. That is, he surprised everybody but Berra.

In a flash Yogi pounced on the ball and fired to third as Hodges came sliding in. The umpire peered into the cloud of dust. "Out!" he shouted, jerking his thumb in the air. The crowd of nearly seventy thousand roared its approval of the fine play.

Then Clem Labine, the Dodger pitcher, came up. Labine dropped another bunt, a good one down the first base line. Again Yogi was on the ball like a tiger. He scooped it up and threw without pause to third. Furillo came barreling in from second. McDougald went down for the tag. "Out!" cried the umpire again, and another roar from the appreciative crowd sounded throughout the Stadium.

Then leadoff man Junior Gilliam lifted a high pop foul behind the plate. Berra took it for the third out, and trotted into the dugout to a wave of enthusiastic applause.

The Yankees went on to win, 9–5, and capture their fifth straight World Championship, unprecedented in major league history.

A combination of old age and the Cleveland Indians finally caught up with the Yankees in 1954. Rizzuto, thirty-six years old, hit an abysmal .195. Veteran hurlers Reynolds and Lopat won twenty-five games between them. These final remnants of the pre-Stengel Yankees hurt the club, but more than anything else was the fact that for once the Indians didn't fade in the stretch. Cleveland came up with 111 victories that year to beat the Yankees by eight games.

That the Yankees hung in the race until early September could be attributed in good part to Berra. Adding something new to his batting repertoire—hitting to the opposite field—he hit .307, with 22 homers and 125 runs batted in. Thus, despite the Indians' pennant, Yogi won the Most Valuable Player Award again, narrowly beating out Larry Doby and Bobby Avila of the pennant winners.

"Take him out and we fall apart," said Casey Stengel one blazing summer day in 1955. The Yankees were locked in a desperate struggle with the Indians and White Sox. No team could keep a strong hold on first place. Meanwhile, suffering from half a dozen bruises and sores, racked with exhaustion, Yogi played day after day to keep the Yankees in the race. He smacked game-winning hits, babied the pitchers, threw out runners.

"That feller back there, Mr. Berra, he's holding us together," Stengel said.

As the race entered the season's final two weeks, Cleveland held a one-game lead over the Yankees. The Red Sox were in town for a series in the Stadium.

"We gotta win the opener," Stengel said in the pre-game discussion. "We fall two games behind we got troubles."

Whitey Ford started for the Bombers, against big Frank Sullivan of the Red Sox. In the fifth, the game scoreless, an aching Yogi dragged himself to the batter's box with two on and two out. Sullivan came in with a low fast ball. Yogi's bat flashed, and like a golf shot the ball went on a line into the right-field seats. That put the Yankees ahead, 3–0.

The Red Sox came back, chased Ford, and tied the score in the eighth.

In the ninth, with Ellis Kinder hurling in relief for Boston, Hank Bauer homered. Yogi followed right behind him with his second homer of the afternoon. That sewed up a 5–3 victory.

"See what I mean about the guy?" Stengel said afterward. "He could be dead but he still wins 'em for you."

Coupled with a Cleveland defeat, the Yankees' victory put them in first place by two percentage points, and they went on to capture the pennant.

That was the year the Dodgers finally broke the Yankee jinx and beat them in the World Series.

But for Yogi, who hit .417 in the Series, the year ended in complete bliss. For the third time in five years he was voted the Most Valuable Player in the American League, joining a very select group of major league all-time greats. In the American League only Jimmy Foxx and Joe DiMaggio had won the MVP three times (later Mantle was to do it). In the National League it was only Stan Musial and Roy Campanella, who had also won his third that year of 1955.

For years there had been comparisons made of these two great catchers. They were the best in baseball. There was no doubt about that, or the fact that they were among the all-time great receivers of the game. But which one was better than the other? The argument, like most such arguments, had no answer. Each man had his adherents among fans, the press, and baseball experts. Statistically there was little to choose from. Berra had a slightly higher batting average, Campanella more homers. Campanella struck out more, but more bases were stolen on Berra.

Berra fans would say he batted in more runs, and Campanella's would argue that he was four years older and, being a Negro, didn't get to play in the majors until he was twenty-seven, where Berra was a Yankee at twenty-one.

As for the intangibles, each man was considered a master at handling pitchers, at calling the signals, as a field general. Perhaps Berra could field a bunt better, but then maybe Campanella was better under a foul pop-up. It was really a moot question. Year after year each man cemented his own position among the superstars of baseball.

Before Yogi tossed aside the catching tools some years later, he set a few more records next to his name in the books. He was the highest paid catcher of all time, set a major league record of 358 lifetime homers for a catcher, tied his own American League record by hitting 30 homers again in one season (1956), and set a major league record by going through 148 consecutive games (July 28, 1957–May 10, 1959) and 950 chances without an error. He also set a long paragraph full of World Series records.

When Elston Howard came up in 1955, as the Yankees' first Negro player, Berra began to make room for him by switching part time to the outfield. Gradually he made way for the new star. He in fact welcomed the occasional change, since playing the outfield gave his catching-weary bones a chance to rest.

At the end of 1963, when manager Ralph Houk, who had taken over the reins from Stengel in 1961, became the club's general manager, Yogi was named as the new skipper of the Yankees.

The romance lasted just one season. Yogi won the pennant, but lost the World Series. The Yankees let him go after that 1964 season. Some said Yogi was treated unfairly, after all his years of service; others said he couldn't manage a major league team because he was too nice, too friendly with his old mates and couldn't instill discipline.

In any case, when the Yankees fired him, his old boss Casey Stengel hired him. Stengel, manager of the New York Mets, put Yogi to work as a coach, working with the pitchers and the catchers, and handling traffic at the first base box during the games.

There he stood, through a succession of Mets' managers, still amiable of nature, still good for a funny remark or as the butt of one, with an untarnishable record as one of the all-time heroic figures behind the mask. All Yogi was waiting for, as the 1968 season drew to a close, was the eventual call from the Hall of Fame.

2

THOSE who were fortunate enough to witness the event, either at the ball park or on their television sets, would in all likelihood never completely forget it. Even now, two decades later, nostalgic lovers of baseball reach back into the dim corners of their memories to talk about the night Roy Campanella came to play with the Brooklyn Dodgers.

That evening, early in July, was calm and warm. A yellow moon hung limply over Ebbets Field, its glow pale against the brilliance of the floodlights atop the grandstand. The outfield grass gleamed emerald green in the artificial brightness. The shrill cries of the hot dog and the scorecard vendors rose over the excited mutterings of the huge throng. Then came a hush as organist Gladys Gooding began the national anthem, and the opening bars blared forth from the loudspeaker system.

As the fans rose in silence, many had their eyes now on the figure at home plate, standing there, mask tucked under his left arm, cap held over his heart, looking out at the flag flying high over center field.

He was round and solid, and being not overly tall—several inches under six feet, in fact—appeared almost roly-poly, like a beardless Santa Claus in baseball uniform. His face was relaxed and pleasant. His skin was dark brown. In July of 1948, this made him more than just an oddity in baseball; he was a pioneer. Just one year earlier Jackie Robinson had made baseball history by becoming the first Negro to play in the major leagues. Now Roy Campanella had followed him onto the Dodgers.

Called up from the St. Paul farm team that very day, he was put immediately into uniform, that number 39 that was to become so familiar and dear to Dodger fans, so much a symbol of Dodger power and supremacy, so much a part of their colorful history in Brooklyn.

As he stood there at the plate, listening and waiting, Roy Campanella might well have reflected on the strange and difficult paths he had followed to reach Ebbets Field —paths that so often seemed to lead nowhere but to the closed doors of bigotry. But Roy was one of those rare men endowed, perhaps fortunately, perhaps unfortunately, with limitless faith and patience. And now, now he could at least look back with a knowledge and pride of accomplishment reached by few men in their lifetime.

Life was not easy for many Americans in the early 1930's, a time of great economic depression. For the son of an Italian fruit peddler and a Negro mother, life was even more difficult than for most. Though they might have had little else, however, the Campanellas had faith in abundance. With this, and generous portions of love and understanding, John and Ida Campanella brought Roy, his older brother and two older sisters through the most difficult years.

In the long afternoons of spring and summer, as his

father pushed the umbrellaed cart through the streets of Philadelphia, hawking the fruits and vegetables, young Roy played baseball on the sandlots. Even at ten he was husky and stronger than the other boys and, because of his size and his willingness, was invariably chosen to be catcher.

Willing he certainly was, more than willing. He would gladly have played anywhere on the field. Roy loved baseball with a happy passion. At Asa Packer Elementary School, in the Nicetown section of Philadelphia, Roy's grades were above average, but he was not an inspired student. His heart belonged to baseball.

He played anytime, anywhere and any position. Usually selected for catcher, he could throw so hard that sometimes he was asked to play the outfield, even pitch.

"I don't care where I play, fellas," he would pipe up in his thin, high voice, a trademark in later years. "Just let me play."

By the time he was fourteen, baseball had become more than just a sandlot sport to Roy; it was the dominating influence in his life. At that age he was already playing senior amateur baseball with the Nicetown Giants, a team supported by Forrest White, publisher of the Philadelphia *Independent,* a Negro newspaper.

Roy was a boy among men there, pitted against players in their late teens and even early twenties. What's more, he was playing better than most of them.

Such baseball heroics did not go unnoticed in the Nicetown community, which supported its amateur league enthusiastically. Roy was a local celebrity, although, modest as he was, wrapped up completely in playing as he was, he didn't realize it.

Soon enough, however, Roy's brother Larry learned of his kid brother's reputation. Twenty-five years old, married, and a rabid baseball fan, he had bought Roy his first good catcher's mitt, and he saw now an opportunity

43

for him to make some money out of baseball in the near future.

John Campanella was less than enthusiastic, however. To him, all this fuss about Roy's ability as a baseball player was sheer foolishness.

Around the Campanella dinner table one night, Larry brought up the subject.

"Y'know, Pop," he said, "Roy's got a good chance to make a nice buck out of baseball."

Mr. Campanella halted a forkful of spaghetti halfway to his mouth to stare at his son. "He's gonna make money playing this baseball? You tell me how."

"Playing semipro. Weekends, maybe all summer. And later on, who knows?"

"I know, that's who knows," said Mr. Campanella. "And what's Roy gonna do when there's no baseball, eh? He's gonna sell bananas off a pushcart like his old man, eh? No, better he forget this foolishness and do good in school, learn a trade."

"Where's your faith, Pop?" Larry chided him, but laughing. "If Roy's good enough, maybe someday he'll even play in the big leagues."

Mr. Campanella put his fork down in exasperation. "Faith? I got faith, Larry. But I also got eyes in my head to see. I don't know too much about this baseball, Larry, but this much I know. I never heard of no colored boy playing baseball in the big leagues."

Twin black Cadillacs sped along the highway toward Beach Haven, New Jersey, bearing the Bacharach Giants baseball team. A semipro, barnstorming aggregation of Negro players, the Bacharachs were a hardened group of travelers. The entire team and all it owned fit into the two cars. In their league, there was little room for spare men, spare parts, coaches or trainers. This was "no play, no pay" baseball.

On the back seat of the lead car, next to catcher-manager Tom Dixon, Roy sat dozing, letting the darkness take him as the big Cadillac sped smoothly through the night. Half-daydreaming, his mind whirled on the wonderment of his being there. These were men he was with, professionals, really, on a hot-shot team famous throughout the East Coast. And here he was, fifteen years old, traveling toward his first game of baseball for money.

It had all happened so swiftly. He had been playing that summer for an American Legion team as well as the Nicetown Giants. He had noticed, that particular Saturday afternoon, the big Cadillac parked at the curb near the field, but paid it no special mind. After the game, however, the man in the car had called him over, introduced himself as Tom Dixon, and asked did he want to play with the Bacharach Giants.

Join the Bacharachs! Everybody had heard of the Bacharachs! Then Dixon had driven him home to talk to his parents. They had required a good deal of persuasion.

As he sat in Dixon's car now, relaxing against the deep cushions, Roy closed his eyes and recalled the scene: Dixon talking softly, convincingly to his parents, telling them he would look after him, see that he got his sleep, ate properly, went to church on Sunday; his mother worrying, unsure about the consequences of sending her boy out into the world of men. The Bacharachs played only on weekends, but they covered a lot of territory, and Roy would be away from home from Friday to Monday.

Finally Dixon had won his point. And, after all, the Bacharachs would be paying Roy thirty-five dollars for his weekend's work. Thirty-five dollars! Why, that was more money than his father earned in a whole week sometimes!

That had been just one week ago. It still seemed like a dream. Suddenly Roy felt nervous butterflies in his stomach. Was he really good enough to play in this fast, semipro company? His eyes opened and he stared out into the darkness, listening to the hum of the tires on the highway, the heavy breathing of the slumbering men around him.

Then he felt an elbow poke him in the ribs. "Better get some sleep, boy," Tom Dixon said. "You got a hard weekend coming."

Actually, Roy thought he would see little action at first, figuring that he had been hired as an eventual replacement for Dixon, who was aging. At the Beach Haven ball park next day, however, as he was helping to unload equipment from the car, Dixon said to him:

"Might as well put the tools on now and catch batting practice, kid. That way you'll get the feel of the park."

Roy stared at him in amazement. "You mean I'm gonna play today?"

Dixon grunted. "That's what you're here for, ain't it?"

Nervously Roy began to strap on his shin guards. He hadn't bargained for such quick action. He had hoped to sort of ease into things, get used to his teammates and the routine of the club before being called upon to work a game.

His gear on, he waddled to the plate, motioned for the first Bacharach hitter to step in, and nodded to the pitcher to get working.

At once everything fell into place. With his catching tools on and the big mitt on his left hand, Roy felt a surge of confidence. "Heck," he said to himself, "this is no different than catching for Nicetown, or the Legion. These guys are just older, that's all."

As each Bacharach hitter stepped up and took his swings, Roy's confidence grew. Soon he was chatting

46

away, as was his custom, in that thin, high, piping voice, needling the batters, cajoling them.

"Swing that bat, man," he urged each of them, "swing it. That little ball ain't gonna bite you."

The Bacharachs warmed to his constant good-natured banter, and by the time the game began, they had accepted him as one of their own.

Roy's debut in semiprofessional baseball was quietly successful. He performed no great batting heroics. On the other hand, his defensive skills played an important part in the Bacharach victory. For a fifteen-year-old playing in a fast league, he showed amazing poise and confidence, handling his pitcher like a professional. Furthermore, in the early innings the first Beach Haven runner to reach base tried to steal on the kid catcher; Roy threw him out by five feet. Thereafter no liberties were taken with his arm.

In the rather loosely organized precincts of the semipro and professional Negro baseball leagues, a good young prospect quickly drew attention. Formal contracts were extremely rare; players went from team to team as the market sought them, although club owners did try to keep raiding to a minimum. Soon, therefore, word of the Bacharachs' brilliant young catcher got around. By the summer of that year, 1937, Roy had accepted an offer from the Baltimore Elites.

This was big-time Negro baseball—the Negro National League. They were relegated perhaps to second- and third-rate ball parks, performing before largely segregated crowds, operating with well-worn equipment and very little money, but they were thoroughly professional. There were ballplayers in the Negro leagues many times better than the average major leaguer. Avid baseball followers and sportswriters were aware of, and sometimes had seen, such legendary athletes as catcher Josh Gibson and pitcher Satchel Paige. But integrated baseball was still ten years away. By the time it came, Gibson was gone. Paige, seemingly ageless, spent a number of years bouncing around the majors long after he should have retired to a rocking chair—and still performed amazing feats on the mound from time to time.

None of this was in Roy's mind, of course, at the time he accepted the Elites' offer. As far as he was concerned, this was as far as he could ever go in baseball. He didn't think beyond that at all. For one thing, it was fantastic that a fifteen-year-old should be hired as the Elites' first-string catcher. For another, young as he was, he realized that he had many years ahead of him to grow in Negro baseball, and he knew that many of the top stars earned salaries comparable to those paid major leaguers. In any case, he would have played for nothing except the thrill of wearing the Elites' uniform.

That summer of 1937 was idyllic for Roy; he lived in a dream, playing baseball virtually every day—and being paid for it as well. True, the schedule of the Elites was a grueling one, but a strong, growing athlete like Roy took it in stride.

In order to make money, Negro teams were forced to adopt rugged schedules, at the same time keeping expenses down by allowing for minimum comforts. In a big blue bus with creaking springs and smoking radiator, the Elites lived on the road. Rarely did they play in the same city two days in succession. They played a game, often two games, one day, got back on their bus, drove to another city, perhaps sleeping on the bus, and played the next day—often enough another doubleheader.

That bus was their home, their dressing room, their restaurant, their hotel. The players lived on sandwiches and thermos jugs of coffee day after day. It was a rare evening indeed when manager Biz Mackey could look at his schedule and call a halt for dinner. And dinner for the Elites did not mean entering some first-class restaurant for a good meal, white cloths on the table and bowing waiters. Dinner meant stopping at some greasy back-road diner that allowed Negroes on the premises. Often these were places with special "Coloreds Only" signs, which meant third-rate food at first-rate prices.

Still, the players survived. They had to. There was no alternative if you were colored and wanted to play professional baseball. Whiners and complainers and weaklings didn't last long in Negro baseball. You didn't sit out a charley horse or a spike wound or the chronic muscular aches and pains common to all professional athletes. You had to play because the team had few bench warmers. They couldn't afford to pay men to sit on the bench. If a player was injured—well, the manager always carried a first-aid kit and a bottle of liniment.

Every player knew that were he injured seriously enough to warrant being replaced, chances were he would be replaced permanently. There was no future for the fragile in this league.

Roy was one of the very few utility men carried by the Elites. He didn't catch every game because of his inexperience, and because manager Mackey was also a catcher, and he liked to play. However, as soon as the Elites' skipper saw that his young protégé could hit the best of the league's pitchers, he assigned him to the outfield when he himself was catching.

By late summer, Roy was the *wunderkind* of the Negro National League. He was breaking the fences with his smashing drives, handling his pitchers like an old pro, cutting down brazen base runners with lightning throws. The league buzzed with excitement about him. The crowds loved him. The Negro newspapers carried his exploits. Fans flocked into the ball parks to see this amazing fifteen-year-old squat behind the plate and call the signals for a pitcher possibly old enough to be his father.

It was far from easy for the youngster. In addition to the usual hardships of the schedule, there were the pitchers he had to handle. Anything went in this league. Spit balls, shine balls, emery balls—pitchers could and did use all of them. They nicked the ball with a belt buckle, moistened it, rubbed all sorts of strange preparations on it. The ball fluttered and spun and dipped and broke every which way. Roy caught them all, and his fingers paid the price, in bruises and sprains and broken bones.

He learned baseball that summer, the hardest way a man could learn it, and he was yet years away from being a man.

When he had to leave the team that September to return to school, Roy did so with heavy heart. Having tasted glory and adventure and the sporting life, school was now drudgery. Last week he had hit a scorching double off the great Satchel Paige—how could he be content now sitting with boys and girls his own age and worrying about who started the French Revolution?

Nevertheless, there he was. He applied himself and maintained his good grades. He was that kind of boy.

In November, just before Roy's sixteenth birthday, Tom Wilson, the Elites' owner, came to call on the Campanellas. He got directly to the point. He wanted Roy to quit school and join the team in Nashville the following month when they began training for the 1938 season.

John and Ida Campanella were dead against it. They wanted Roy to finish high school, get a diploma. But Wilson was persuasive.

"And then what?" he asked them. "What kind of job could Roy get? Porter at the railroad station? Factory hand maybe, with no future, no chance? I'll pay him ninety dollars a month to start, and on top of that he's his own man. He gets a respect and a popularity he can't get anyplace else. You see that already, don't you?"

There was no denying the truth of Wilson's arguments. Ninety dollars a month, and his expenses paid, was excellent money in 1937. Equally persuasive was the fact that the Campanellas were indeed proud of Roy. Neighbors and friends talked about him glowingly. He was indeed quite the young hero in the Nicetown community. And so John and Ida Campanella saw a future perhaps beyond the usual limits color set for the great majority of boys like him in those years.

Now, in the spring of 1938, baseball became all things in Roy's life. He caught every game for the Elites, including both ends of doubleheaders. His capacity for work was boundless, his enthusiasm unquenchable. He twittered and chirped like a bird behind the plate, yelling encouragement to his teammates, gossiping with and gently needling the opposition.

His stature as a player grew by leaps and bounds. In his second year with the Elites his pay was raised to one hundred twenty dollars a month. He was seventeen years old—and being talked about, written about as a second Josh Gibson. He was invited to play winter ball in the Puerto Rican League, traveling the Caribbean–South American circuit, making baseball a twelve-month proposition for him.

His life was forming a pattern. He was earning money, respect, fame. Through it all he retained his basic good humor and humility. He carried a Bible in his suitcase, and wherever his travels took him, he found a church on Sunday morning. And when he was nineteen, he found a wife, a girl named Ruthe.

He was a happy young man as the spring of 1941 blossomed, supremely content with the shape his world was taking. He would have been well satisfied to let it

51

continue in such fashion, but events outside his life began to intrude.

War was raging in Europe, and the United States began drafting men into the armed services. In April, Roy was called up by his draft board. He passed his physical, and was told to stand by. However, since he was married, and now had a child, he was told he could stay out of the army if he found a job in a defense plant.

Though he had no skills for such work, Roy tried. At first all he could get was a job as a porter, sweeping out at the Bendix Aviation plant. Later he found a job helping to make armor plate for tanks. After a year at defense work, his draft board reclassified him, deferring him from military service because he was a married man with children—he now had two.

With the reclassification came the board's permission to play baseball.

Happily, Roy rejoined the Elites. Soon, however, friction developed between him and owner Tom Wilson, over Wilson's refusal to let him earn extra money playing exhibition games for an all-star team. Several months later, therefore, when he received an attractive offer from the new Mexican League, he left the Elites.

For two years he lived like a king in Mexico. He made more money than ever before, was treated royally by the owners of the Monterrey team, and regarded as a national hero by the avid Mexican baseball fans.

Then, in October of 1945, he was preparing for a season of winter ball in Venezuela when he received a phone call from Mrs. Effa Manley, owner of the Newark Eagles. A good Negro team, the Eagles' star performer was a fireballing young pitcher named Don Newcombe.

"Roy," Mrs. Manley said, "we're getting together an all-star team to play an exhibition series of five games against a team of major leaguers. You interested?"

"Sure," Roy said. He wasn't due in Venezuela for

several weeks, and the idea of playing against major leaguers appealed to him. According to Mrs. Manley, the other team would have such stars as Ralph Branca, Hal Gregg, Whitey Kurowski, Eddie Stanky and Tommy Holmes.

A doubleheader at Ebbets Field opened the exhibition series. The Dodgers' Hal Gregg beat Roy's team in the first game, 4–3. The second game was called because of darkness and rain with the score tied, 1–1.

Then the series switched to the Eagles' field in Newark. Just before game time, as he was waddling to the plate, Roy heard his name being called. He turned and saw that Charley Dressen, a coach for the Brooklyn Dodgers and manager of the all-stars, was beckoning to him.

He walked over to him. "What's up, Charley?" he asked.

"Wait for me after the game, Campy," Dressen said. "I want to talk to you."

"What about?"

"Not now. There's no time. Just meet me later, outside the players' entrance. Don't forget."

Roy shrugged and went back to the plate. A moment later the game started, and he dismissed Charley Dressen from his mind. He didn't think it could be very important, anyway.

Of course, what Dressen actually did have to say was of vital, monumental importance. He had brought an invitation from Branch Rickey, owner of the Brooklyn Dodgers. Would Roy like to come around next day and have a chat? Roy would indeed.

Still, the interview was a strange one. As Roy sat in Rickey's office, his puzzlement growing, the Dodger chief prattled on about a new Negro League he was thinking of forming, and a new team called the Brooklyn Bombers.

He was very vague, talking on and on behind a cloud of blue cigar smoke. When Roy left the office an hour later, he hardly had a clue as to what it was all about, except that Rickey had asked him not to sign any contracts for the following year until he heard from him.

A week later, he was sitting in the lobby of the Woodside Hotel in New York with a group of Negro players, all bound for Venezuela. Sprawled in the overstuffed leather chairs, chatting away with small talk, were such stars as Sam Jethroe, Jackie Robinson, Buck Leonard, Marv Williams and Roy.

Suddenly the music that had been blaring forth from the radio cut out, and a voice broke in with a news bulletin: "The Brooklyn Dodger baseball club announced today that Jackie Robinson, star infielder for the Kansas City Monarchs of the Negro National League, has signed a Brooklyn contract. It is expected that he will play with the Montreal Royals next season. . . ."

Pandemonium broke loose in the hotel lobby. The players swarmed around Robinson, clapping him on the back, wringing his hand, asking him how it had all happened. The first Negro to play in organized baseball!

Later, when he had time to think about it, Roy realized the full implications of Robinson's signing with the Dodgers. At first he didn't dare believe it, but then, carefully examining the evidence, he saw that it must be so. Rickey had just been sizing him up personally. There wasn't going to be a Brooklyn Bombers. Rickey had him in mind for the Dodgers!

On the plane down to Venezuela he discussed his thoughts with Robinson, who agreed that it was likely. "But it's going to be rough, Roy," Robinson cautioned. "A lot will depend on how I make out."

Tough it was, indeed.

By the time Roy returned from South America and got the call from Branch Rickey, Robinson was already in Florida and having trouble with segregationists. Thus, though the Dodgers did want to send him to spring training with Montreal and Robinson, they felt it was wiser to send him elsewhere.

Roy was in the Dodger offices in Brooklyn when they were trying to place him with a farm team. These were agonizing moments for him. As much as he wanted to break into organized baseball, this business of being tossed about like an unwanted old has-been was degrading. First Montreal couldn't take him. Then Bob Finch, a Dodger executive, phoned Danville, Illinois. They wouldn't take Roy.

Sitting there, he felt the anger and the resentment rise within him. Such feelings were alien to him. He didn't like having them, and he didn't like what was causing them. Why should he sit there and be subjected to such treatment, when he could remain in the Negro National League, or play Mexican ball, where he was respected and treated with dignity? He didn't need favors from anybody, didn't need to hang around this office, like a beggar, hat in hand, hoping for a kind word from a white man!

He was on the verge of getting up and walking out when Finch began talking to him, explaining that these were the problems they all had to expect, and though he realized how humiliating this might be for Roy, he hoped Roy would stick it out and help the Dodgers break down all the old prejudices.

Roy agreed. It was true enough. After all the years, the decades of segregationist tradition in baseball, could he expect to be greeted with open arms everywhere?

Gratified, Finch then placed a call to Nashua, New Hampshire. In a few minutes he hung up and turned to Roy, his face wreathed in smiles.

"We did it!" he said. "I spoke to Buzzy Bavasi, Nashua's general manager. A great guy. He said he didn't care if you were green with orange spots or had two heads. If you could hit, he wanted you." Finch shook Roy's hand. "I'll arrange the ticket and some expense money," he said. "You'll like it in Nashua. Good manager, there, name of Walt Alston."

Bavasi, of course, later became vice-president of the Dodgers, and Alston the very successful manager.

In Nashua, Roy teamed up with his old friend from the Newark Eagles, pitcher Don Newcombe. Together they helped Nashua to a second-place finish in the New England League, Roy hitting .290 and batting in 96 runs. He led the league in put-outs for a catcher, with 187, and assists, with 64. He and Newcombe were subjected to a certain amount of racial bench-jockeying from opposing teams, but they had expected far worse. Their own team-mates accepted them calmly, and the people of Nashua, largely French-Canadian in origin, treated them warmly.

The Dodgers realized Roy was far too good for Class B baseball. The following year he was promoted, with Newcombe, to Montreal, as Robinson joined the Dodgers, becoming the first Negro to play in the major leagues.

Again Roy had an outstanding year. After hitting .300 most of the season, he tailed off at the end and finished with a .273 average, 13 homers and 75 runs batted in. Again he led his league in put-outs and assists, and this time in fielding average, with .988.

There was no question about his being ready for the Dodgers now. But crusading Branch Rickey had another job for him. He wanted him to start the season with the St. Paul farm team, to break the color line in the American Association.

Roy was disappointed. But he had tremendous respect for Rickey, and his efforts in behalf of Negro athletes. In his heart he knew he would be recalled as soon as Rickey thought the time was ripe.

On the night of June 30, 1948, in Toledo, Roy collected a single, a double and a home run, and caught both ends of the twi-night doubleheader. In the dressing room afterward Walter Alston, now managing the Saints, gave Roy the news he had been waiting for. "The Dodgers want you, right away," he said.

Now here he was, in Ebbets Field at last, hanging out the sign to Ralph Branca for the first pitch of the game, the first pitch he would receive as a major league catcher. He settled down and went to work.

The game was a scoreless tie when he came to bat in the second inning. The crowd buzzed with excitement; much had been heard about Campanella.

He took Andy Hansen's first pitch for a ball. He took ball two, then a strike. Hansen came back with a fast ball. Roy swung—there was a sharp crack, a shout from the stands. The ball jumped like a bullet, on a line toward right center field. It hit the wall sharply, ricocheted off. By the time Whitey Lockman retrieved it and threw to second, Roy was there standing up with a double.

Two innings later he cracked a line drive single off Giant relief pitcher Sheldon Jones. Later he flied out, but closed out the night's work with another single. Despite Roy's three hits, the Dodgers lost, 6–4, and dropped to last place.

The next day against the Giants he continued his hammering. With a walk, two singles and a triple he gave the Dodgers their first victory in a week. Then, incredibly, he surpassed his first two efforts in the third game. He hit a single and two tremendous homers into the upper left-field stands for another win.

Baseball had never seen a major league debut to match it. Nine hits and a walk in his first thirteen trips to the plate. With two straight victories and the fresh impetus provided by Roy's hitting and catching, the Dodgers began to move. They won sixteen of their next nineteen games, climbed out of the cellar, into the first division, and began to challenge for the league lead.

Roy's hitting suffered in the latter part of his rookie season with the Dodgers, but his defensive skills never failed him. Adventurous base runners quickly learned they were no match for his arm. At one point twelve straight runners were cut down at second before a successful steal was made against him.

The Dodgers didn't quite have it that year. They finished third. Roy hit .258, with 9 homers and 45 runs batted in.

With Roy filling in a damaging gap in the Dodger lineup, manager Barney Shotton was able to shift Gil Hodges to first base and give the team a new look. To open the 1949 season he had Hodges at first, Robinson at second, Pee Wee Reese at shortstop, Spider Jorgensen at third. Duke Snider in center field, Carl Furillo in right and Gene Hermanski in left made up the outfield. The pitching staff was strong, with Erv Palica, Preacher Roe, Ralph Branca and Carl Erskine. And shortly after opening day, Don Newcombe joined the club.

On opening day they beat the Giants, 10–3, and they were off and running. By July 1 it was apparent that the pennant race would be a duel between the Dodgers and the Cardinals. It was apparent, too, that Roy Campanella was the best catcher in the league. So firmly had he established himself that Billy Southworth, manager of the National Leaguers for the All-Star classic, picked him to catch most of the game, though the fans had voted for Andy Seminick of the Phillies.

The battle between the Dodgers and Cardinals raged on all summer. Every game was a vital one. At one point Roy was beaned by Bill Werle, the Pirates' left-hander.

He was rushed to the hospital, where x-rays disclosed no serious injury. "Just a day or two of rest and you'll be all right," the doctor said.

"Rest?" Roy exclaimed. "Man, I got no time to rest." Despite the doctor's warnings Roy signed himself out of the hospital and rejoined the Dodgers at once. He didn't miss a game.

It took a ten-inning, 9–7 victory on the last day of the season to give the Dodgers the pennant—but win it they did. And though they lost the World Series to the Yankees, the players felt they were beginning a new era of Dodger dominance.

It was a fine year for Roy. He hit .287, leading the league's catchers in every department—batting, fielding percentage and put-outs.

His catching in the World Series opened the eyes of the Yankees, too, and they compared Roy favorably with their own great receiver, Yogi Berra. Phil Rizzuto in particular had high praise for Roy—with good reason. In the fourth game Roy picked him off third base. Rizzuto couldn't get over it for days. "I can't understand it," he said over and over again. "That never happened to me before in my life. Campanella made it look easy!"

Roy came back with another fine year in 1950, hitting .281, with 31 homers and 89 runs batted in. But 1950 was the year of the Philadelphia Whiz Kids, and the young Phillies took the pennant.

The incredible 1951 season began with the Dodgers moving quickly into first place, and their arch rivals, the Giants, losing eleven straight. With such a start, no one could have predicted that these two teams would be at each other's throats at the season's gripping climax.

Riding high with the Dodgers was Roy, reaching new heights of performance. Early in May, in a two-game series at Ebbets Field, he personally demolished the Braves. He won the opening game for Preacher Roe, 4–3, with two singles, a double and a home run. The next day three singles and a home run gave Newcombe a 5–3 victory.

Through late spring and early summer he maintained a savage pace. Late-inning, game-winning hits became his specialty. Two days in a row he beat the Cardinals with a tie-breaking home run. In a four-game series with the Giants he got seven hits in sixteen trips, including two homers; the Dodgers won three out of four.

Then Eddie Miksis of the Cubs spiked him in the hand. For two days he fretted on the sidelines, until, against doctor's orders, he came back with the wound still open. Pressing a rubber sponge into his palm, he grabbed a bat and rapped out two doubles to drive home four runs in a 6–4 victory.

There appeared to be no stopping him. Every time he walked up to the plate he was a threat to break open the game. In late innings, when the Dodgers were trailing, tension mounted in the ball park; there was the feeling that if Campy got one more chance to bat, he might start a winning rally. Or, if the game were close enough, he might win it himself with one of his clutch home runs.

In mid-July he went on a rampage that gave him 11 hits in 23 trips. Five of the hits were homers, the last a tenth-inning blast that beat the Cubs, 6–3.

One of his typically heroic feats took place in St. Louis, a week after the Chicago series. In the opening game at Sportsman's Park, the Cardinals jumped off to a quick 3–1 lead. But in the fourth inning Roy doubled home two runs, to tie the score. St. Louis came back to open up a 9–3 lead, and even die-hard Dodger fans counted this game lost.

They had forgotten about Campanella.

After the Dodgers picked up a run in the sixth, Roy started a two-run rally in the seventh with another double, and the score now was 9–6. Three more runs in the eighth tied the game.

Duke Snider opened the Dodger ninth with a walk. Del Rice, the Red Bird catcher, tried to pick him off, threw wildly, and the Duke wound up on second. Now the Cardinals' reluctant strategy was to purposely walk Gil Hodges, to get to Campanella. Despite the threat Roy represented, he was not a fast runner; the Cardinals hoped he would hit the ball on the ground for a double play.

Roy promptly hit a home run to break up the game.

The league couldn't fight this kind of clutch hitting. By August the Dodgers were ten games in front, sailing smoothly toward the pennant. Then, on August 5, during a game with the Giants, Whitey Lockman tried to score from first on a double by Willie Mays and crashed into Campanella, sending him sprawling into the dirt. Roy remained in the game, but for the next few days complained about a soreness in his elbow that was affecting his swing.

Finally, x-rays were taken, revealing bone chips resulting from the collision. The doctors insisted Roy take a week off and rest the elbow. He stayed away four days, then put the tools back on and returned to the lineup.

While he was playing at less than total efficiency the Giants began an incredible drive. In mid-August they won sixteen straight games, pulling to within six games of the Dodgers. Still, with barely four weeks remaining in the season, no one gave them a chance to overtake the league leaders.

Then Campanella was hurt again—beaned in Chicago by a pitch thrown by Turk Lown. He missed another five games; his face was still bruised and swollen when he returned, but he was urgently needed. In his absence the Dodgers' lead had dwindled to a mere three games.

Slowly, inexorably, the Giants whittled away at that margin. Until finally the Dodgers had only a half-game lead, with three games to play, while the Giants had two.

The Giants were in Boston with a day off when the Dodgers opened their season's final series against Philadelphia. The Whiz Kids, though out of the pennant race, relished the idea of being in on the climax, cast in the role of decisive opponents for the Dodgers.

They clobbered ace Carl Erskine in the first game, and the unbelievable had happened. The once "invincible" Dodger lead—at one point thirteen and a half games—had vanished completely. They were tied with the Giants for first place.

Each team had two games left now. The Giants were confident, eager, loose. Win or lose they would come out heroes, deliverers of a miracle, or a near miracle. On the other hand, the Dodgers were backed into a corner; and pros though they were, they felt the tension and the pressure.

The next day the Giants won in Boston, and Newcombe pitched a shutout in Philadelphia.

They were down to the final hours now. Each team played that final game with one eye on the scoreboard.

In Boston, the Giants took the lead. In Philadelphia, the Dodgers were losing, 6–1, as they came to bat in the fourth inning. Then Campanella stepped in and hit a tremendous blast to deep right center field. Racing desperately, he rounded first, tore for second, rounded the bag, kept going, charged for third and made it with a triple—but halfway down from second he had begun to hobble like a horse pulling up lame.

A few moments later he scored on a single, limping all the way down the line and into the dugout.

Three more runs came across for the Dodgers in the fifth, and the score was 6–5. Campanella was dragging his left leg now as he walked.

As the eighth inning began, the flash came from Boston that the Giants had won, 3–2.

The baseball world concentrated on Philadelphia now. In their dressing room at Boston, the Giants sat in their clubhouse, still in sweat-stained uniforms, listening to a broadcast of the Dodger game.

The Phillies drew ahead, 8–5. It looked like disaster for Brooklyn, but they pushed over three runs in the eighth to tie the score. Neither team could score in the ninth, and the game went into extra innings.

Through the thirteenth inning the tie remained, while the Giants sat nervously in their clubhouse, fidgeting with each pitch, and the hot dog vendors in Shibe Park stopped hawking their wares to watch the game.

For Roy, each inning brought fresh agony. His left leg was a knot of pain that spread with each moment. Hitting was difficult enough; the constant knee-bending behind the plate brought excruciating pain. The manager noticed his predicament, but Roy made no move to complain, and the situation was too tense to allow a second-string catcher to take over.

The first two Dodgers in the top of the fourteenth were retired. Then Jackie Robinson stepped up, hit the first pitch, and smashed it over the left-field wall for a home run.

The Dodgers went wild, jumping up and down in the dugout, rushing out to home plate to greet Robinson. In Boston, a Giant player walked over to the radio and shut it off.

The Phillies went down meekly in their half of the fourteenth, and the 1951 pennant race had ended in a tie. The Giants and Dodgers would have to battle it out in a three-game playoff series.

In the dressing room of the Dodgers before the third game, a grim dialogue was taking place. A split of the first two playoff games once again had narrowed the pennant race to the final hours. It was as though the rest of the schedule had been played for a lark, and the only result that would count was this final one.

Charley Dressen, the team's manager now, was not happy about the Dodgers' situation. He was staring disconsolately at the figure of Campanella, lying on the rubbing table.

"How's it feel, Campy?" he asked.

Roy managed a twisted grin. "I walked in here today. That's more than I figured on being able to do."

Dressen looked inquiringly at team physician Dominic Rossi. The doctor shrugged helplessly. "The thigh muscle is badly knotted. We can tape it, shoot it full of Novocain—and hope it'll hold up."

Campanella sat up. "I can play, Skip. We gotta win this one today."

Dressen sighed wearily. He wanted Roy to play, needed him desperately. But he needed a healthy Roy. Playing that fourteen-inning game, after he'd pulled up lame in the fourth inning, had aggravated the injured muscle. In the first playoff game he was a pitiful sight, batting weakly, his power crippled by the bad leg. Gamely, he ran out the ground ball he tapped out to the infield, bravely he squatted behind the plate, the effort bringing the sweat out on his forehead.

It was no good. He was crippling himself and hurting the team.

He sat out the second contest. For the third, the final game, Dressen wanted him more than ever, because Newcombe was pitching. Roy knew better than anybody how to coax the best possible performance from the sensitive, volatile hurler.

In the dressing room, the Dodger manager decided to postpone his decision until the team took batting practice.

Roy took his place in the cage, some minutes later, and gave it all he had. Biting his lip to mask the pain, he swung gallantly at the serves from the batting practice pitcher. Only one or two did he hit solidly.

"Run one out now, Roy," Dressen said. He was standing at the side of the cage, watching intently.

Campanella hit the next pitch on the ground to the left side and ran down the first base line, trying to hide the limp. He turned around after crossing the bag and trotted back to Dressen.

"See? I can run okay, can't I, Skip?"

"Like a gazelle," Dressen said dryly. "With three legs."

Team captain Reese joined them. "The truth, Campy," Pee Wee said. "We know how much you want to play, and you know how much we want you in there. But if you can't make it, well, it just doesn't make sense to go out there."

Roy hesitated. All his training, all his years of knocking about in the Negro leagues had instilled in him the drive to play every inning of every game unless you were flat on your back. However, this was a different situation, he realized. Stubborn insistence at this point might be more pride than dedication to the team. Winning was all that mattered today, and he had to decide whether he was an asset or a liability in the game.

Finally, he shook his head sorrowfully.

"That's it, then," Dressen said. He put his arm around Roy's shoulder and walked with him back to the dugout.

And so that final game of the titanic Dodger-Giant duel began, with Rube Walker catching Newcombe, Roy on the bench fiercely exhorting the big right-hander inning by inning:

"C'mon, big Newk, hum that pea!"

For a time Newcombe had it all his own way. He

breezed through the first six innings, nursing a 1–0 lead, his fast ball bowling over the Giant hitters.

In the seventh Monte Irvin doubled, moved to third on an infield out and scored on a fly ball by Bobby Thomson.

The Dodgers struck back savagely against Sal Maglie, their perennial archenemy. Four hits, a walk and a wild pitch sent three runs thundering across the plate. Newcombe set the Giants down in order in their half of the eighth, and went into the bottom of the ninth with his 4–1 lead.

The most die-hard of Giant fans sat without hope now. Dodger fans in the stands began whooping it up in anticipation of victory. Even the Dodger players on the bench were forced to restrain themselves from premature celebration.

Many fans began heading for the exits as Al Dark stepped up to lead off the Giants' ninth. They hardly paused when he cracked Newcombe for a single. Don Mueller followed with another single. The moving crowds stopped short, stood on the concrete runways. The game wasn't over yet.

Newcombe bore down, got Irvin on a foul pop fly. But Lockman doubled to score Dark, and now the Giant fans began to leap about and shout with renewed hope. Dodger fans shook their heads—would there never be an easy victory?

With the score 4–2 and men on second and third, a base hit would tie the score.

Here manager Dressen went to the mound and made the decision heard 'round the baseball world—for decades afterward. He pulled Newcombe and waved Ralph Branca in from the bullpen.

As Branca trudged in and took his warm-up tosses, it seemed all of New York had come to a standstill, waiting for him to pitch to Bobby Thomson. All over the great city television sets had been bought, borrowed or rented for this game, planted in offices, in stores, in factories. Every car radio appeared tuned to the game, and from store fronts, loudspeakers blared forth the play-by-play to passers-by on the streets.

As Branca took his final warm-ups, debates were already in progress. Was Dressen wise in removing Newcombe at this point, for Branca? The second guessers would soon have grist for their mill.

Thomson dug in at the plate and Branca pitched. Strike one!

"C'mon, Ralphie baby! C'mon!" Roy breathed through clenched teeth.

Branca wound up and threw to the plate. Thomson swung. A sharp crack of the bat—a million people held their breath, players on both teams leaped off the bench to watch the ball sailing toward left.

Roy clenched his fists tightly and stared in horror. "Sink, you devil, sink!" he cried.

Sink the ball did—but into the left-field stands for a home run—a home run that won the game, the playoff and the 1951 pennant for the New York Giants.

It was an unbelievable finish to an already incredible season.

While the Giants prepared to meet the Yankees in the World Series, Roy sadly set about his postseason business. He had opened a liquor store in the Harlem section of Manhattan, and was planning a barnstorming tour with an all-Negro all-star team in mid-October.

He was bitterly disappointed at losing the pennant, and felt he was partially to blame, sidelined as he was for that final playoff game. He had nothing to be ashamed of, however. Quite the contrary; the Dodgers would never have been pennant contenders without his fabulous performance of 1951. In his finest season yet, he hit .325, fourth highest in the league, 33 homers, and batted in 108 runs.

Moreover, in his three full seasons in the major leagues, he had already carved out a unique record, taking his place among the great catchers of all time. He was the first catcher in baseball history to hit 20 or more homers in three successive seasons: 22, 31, 33. Only one other catcher had ever hit 20 or more homers three times in his entire career—Gabby Hartnett. The Yankees' immortal receiver, Bill Dickey, never hit more than 29 homers in one season, further indication of Campanella's batting prowess.

Defensive skills are of course less measurable, yet baseball experts and the players themselves, in both leagues, considered his work behind the plate, his handling of pitchers, to be faultless, often brilliant. In one department where it was possible to keep statistics, his talent as a receiver was unmatched. In 1951, 45 attempts were made to steal against him; only 15 were successful. This average of one out of three he had maintained since joining the Dodgers. The general average of successful steals in both leagues during that period was six out of ten—just about half the effectiveness averaged by Campanella.

It was small wonder, then, that in November, while on tour, he received a call from Dick Young, eminent sportswriter for the New York *Daily News*.

"Campy," Young said, "I'm calling to tell you that the Baseball Writers Association has just voted you the Most Valuable Player in the National League."

Injuries jinxed Roy the following year. Within the first six weeks of the season he suffered a strained back, a badly injured toe, was hit on the hand by a pitch, jammed his right thumb and received a spike wound in another toe. Then in July a foul tip broke his right hand.

For several days he played, broken hand or no, until the swelling and the pain became unbearable. Finally he submitted to a doctor's examination. He was put in a cast up to his elbow and sidelined for ten days.

He came off the bench after that to hit a home run in the ninth inning, tying the score in Pittsburgh; the Dodgers went on to win in the tenth. Three days later a bases-loaded single in the ninth beat the Cubs, 3–2, and four days after that a grand-slam homer beat the Giants, 7–5.

There were too few such streaks, however. The 1952 season was one of chronic injury for him; he was, after all, thirty years old now, not a youngster anymore. Though a comparative newcomer to major league baseball, he was a veteran of fifteen years of professional baseball, most of those years hard-knock Negro ball. His body bore the ravages of countless collisions at home plate, his legs ached from seasons of pounding the sun-baked diamonds, his hands bore the scars of a thousand foul tips.

He helped the Dodgers to a pennant in 1952, with a .269 average, 22 homers, 97 runs batted in. He was disgusted with his showing, though the cold statistics still put him among the top catchers in both leagues. He worked that winter, keeping in shape, trimming off some excess weight. He wanted the 1953 season to be better than ever.

In excellent shape on opening day, a solid 205 pounds, he promptly began to tear the league apart. As early as the first week in May he had racked up six home runs, batted in twenty-six runs, and was swinging at a .359 average.

The excitement caused by his powerful slugging tended to overshadow his perennial superiority behind the plate. Until one day in May, when Bill Bruton of the Braves stole second. It occurred suddenly to sportswriter

Jerry Mitchell of the *New York Post,* as he saw Bruton on second, that he didn't remember the last time anybody had stolen a base against Roy. He called down to the press box to Allan Roth, the Dodgers' statistician.

"Hey, Al, when was the last time anyone stole a base on Campy?"

Roth looked through his record books. "September 5, 1952. Fifty-one games ago."

Two innings later, Jim Pendleton tried the same trick, but was cut down by a rifle throw from Roy's right arm.

In the press box, Mitchell leaned back and smiled. "That's better. I thought for a minute there Campy was slipping."

Then the Phillies came to Ebbets Field, leading the league. Two days later they left, trailing the Dodgers, victims of Campanella's magic bat. In the Saturday afternoon game opening the series, Roy came to bat in the bottom half of the ninth, the Dodgers trailing, 6–5, a man on first and two out. The great Robin Roberts was on the mound for Philadelphia.

Roy hit his first pitch into the left-field seats for a 7–6 Dodger victory.

In the night game he walloped two more homers to help the Dodgers make it two straight, and creep to within half a game of first place.

The pivotal Sunday game began, the Dodgers' Billy Loes against Karl Drews. The game was a scoreless tie as the Dodgers came to bat in the third inning. Then Snider singled and Robinson walked. Up came Campanella. He let two pitches go by, then smacked a double off the wall for two runs.

His heroics were not yet over. In the fifth inning Reese singled and Snider singled. After Robinson fouled out, Roy slammed his tenth homer of the young season for a 5–0 lead.

70

Loes held it all the way. The Dodgers were in first place.

The way Campanella was going, Dodger pitchers were having a fairly easy time of it, and the team held onto first place against continual threats by the Phillies and the Braves, newly transferred to Milwaukee. Late in May he again beat Robin Roberts with a two-run homer, and next day against the Phillies began the game-winning rally with an eighth-inning double.

"He's just the best catcher there is in baseball," Steve O'Neill, the Phillies' manager, said after that game. "There isn't a thing he doesn't do better than any other catcher in the game, and when you put them all together, there haven't been more than half a dozen catchers as good as Campy in all the years I've been around."

O'Neill, whose baseball career dated back to 1910, shook his head in admiration. "When you watch Campanella work," he said, "you're seeing one of the masters."

On September 6, with the Dodgers riding comfortably on top of the standings, Roy helped the Dodgers massacre the Giants, 16–7, hitting two homers, driving in five runs.

His second homer of the game was his thirty-seventh of the season, tying the all-time homer record for catchers, set by Gabby Hartnett in 1930. His five runs batted in gave him 131, a new record for Brooklyn, and just two shy of the all-time record for catchers set by the Yankees' Bill Dickey.

A week later the Dodgers clinched the pennant. By the time the season was over, he had set three new catching records: 41 homers, 142 runs batted in, and a fielding mark of 807 put-outs. He hit .312 that year, while leading the league's catchers defensively with a .989 percentage.

In the second inning of the first World Series game, Roy was hit on the right hand by a pitch from Allie

Reynolds of the Yankees. That just about finished the Dodgers for the Series. Roy continued to play, but he could hardly grip a bat. The Yankees took the championship in six games.

The baseball writers of America had little trouble choosing the Most Valuable Player in the National League for 1953. Roy won the award easily. Only three other men in league history had ever won the award more than once up to 1953—Rogers Hornsby, Carl Hubbell and Stan Musial. He also received the Sid Mercer Award, as "Player of the Year," from the New York chapter of the Baseball Writers Association.

Roy accepted the Sid Mercer Award in January, before a gathering of baseball writers, players, executives and assorted dignitaries. He made a short speech of acceptance, telling in his own way about his early love for baseball, and how he never dreamed it would be possible to play in the major leagues. He told of his gratitude toward people like Branch Rickey, and his teammates, and how wonderful baseball was to him, enabling him to take care of his family the way he had always hoped he might.

A week later Buzzy Bavasi, Dodger vice-president, received a phone call from Frank Lane, general manager of the Chicago White Sox. "Maybe you'll think I'm crazy," he said, "but as I was driving down to the office this morning I got to thinking what a great speech it was Campanella made. I called because I have to tell you how good it makes me feel to be associated with a game that has produced a guy like Roy Campanella."

The signing of Walter Alston to manage the Dodgers in 1954 heralded a new chapter in the team's history. Ironically, uniting Roy with his first manager in organized baseball also heralded the beginning of the decline of the great catcher.

It began with an injury. Sliding into second base during a game in spring training, he jammed his left hand into the bag and chipped a bone. Typically, he continued to play, right into the start of the regular season. But when he was batting .167 at the end of April, the Dodgers talked him into the operation that doctors had been recommending.

For a brief period after the operation he seemed fine, then a numbness began to creep into his hand. The fourth and fifth fingers wouldn't move properly, and the muscle behind his thumb was stiff.

He could hardly grip a bat—barely hold a fork, for that matter. Yet in July, though hitting .212, he was named to the All-Star team, and insisted on playing, though he would have been excused considering his condition.

"It may be my last one," he said gloomily, "and I intend to catch."

The All-Star Game only confirmed his fear, however, that his career was in jeopardy. In the eighth inning he was relieved, breaking a string of 55 consecutive All-Star innings for him. Until that point he had caught every inning of every All-Star Game since the seventh inning of the 1948 contest—a major league record.

The Dodgers wanted to put him on the disabled list, but he protested that he wanted to play. He couldn't hit, but he could catch, and in truth the Dodgers had no adequate substitute. Thus for the rest of the season he played intermittently, often in pain, swinging the bat with one good hand. He batted .207 that season, with 19 homers, 55 runs batted in. In light of his condition, even that much was a miracle. But without his bat, the Dodgers lost the pennant.

When the season was over he submitted once more to an operation, this time to repair nerves damaged by the bone splinters. The surgery was delicate, requiring four hours of skillful work by an expert neurological team. When it was done, the surgeon expressed his optimism. "There is an excellent chance that Campanella's hand will return to normal," he said.

It was evident in spring training that this was a new Campanella—with the old confidence. He hit the ball all over the field and out of the park. And when opening day came he began blasting homers and driving home the runs as he had in 1953. When he hit like that he carried the rest of the team with him, and this time he carried them not only to the pennant but to a World Series victory over the Yankees and the first World Championship in Brooklyn history.

When the season was done Roy was named "The Comeback Player of the Year" and, for the third time, the Most Valuable Player in the National League, a distinction held at the time by only four other players in history: Musial in the National League, Jimmy Foxx, Joe DiMaggio and Yogi Berra in the American League (later Mickey Mantle became the sixth so honored).

He had hit .318 for the season, with 32 homers and 107 runs batted in.

"He's indestructible!" chortled manager Alston during the World Series.

But only Roy knew that in the latter part of his comeback season, the numbness in his hand had begun to come back, too.

He had played for weeks on sheer nerve. There comes a time for all athletes, however, when sheer nerve is not enough. The body takes over and betrays the will. The pitcher's fast ball loses its hop. The shortstop is half a step off and the ball goes through the hole. The high hard one begins to get by the big slugger. The catcher's hands become stumps.

When Roy Campanella began the 1956 season he was thirty-four years old with almost twenty years of professional baseball behind him. His hands were swollen, pain-racked lumps. The numbness in his left hand was there again, spreading each day. At the base of the thumb of his right hand, loose bone chips from old injuries rattled away and jabbed at him painfully every time he caught a pitch or swung a bat. One hand didn't feel at all; the other felt too much.

He kept a bucket of ice in the dugout. When the pain became unbearable he soaked his hands between innings, then went out and played again.

He continued to play because the Dodgers needed him. Though he was barely hitting above .200, Alston wouldn't bench him. He was the glue that held the Dodgers together. His presence in the lineup gave them confidence. Moreover, his battered hands had no effect on his brilliant handling of pitchers; he was particularly useful breaking in new young pitchers like Roger Craig and Don Bessent.

Crippled as he was, however, he often came up with the clutch hit, and once again he helped the Dodgers win a pennant. He hit only .219 that season, but his 20 homers and 73 runs batted in indicated that many of his blows were key ones.

Once more, when the season was over, he went under the surgeon's scalpel. This time it was to remove the bone chips from his right hand.

It was no use. As soon as he went back to work in 1957 the daily pounding took its toll. He lived with pain. That was it and he had to accept it; his hands were crippled, and if he played they would hurt. It was as simple as that.

Manager Alston had to bench him more often now. Walker sometimes replaced him in the late innings, and Johnny Roseboro was brought up from Montreal to help.

He finished the 1957 season with his lowest total of games caught since his first full season with the Dodgers,

103. He hit .242, with 13 homers and 62 runs batted in. There were two compensations, however. He now had a record lifetime total of 242 homers, five more than the previous major league record, held by Gabby Hartnett. He had also set a new league record by catching more than a hundred games for the ninth straight season.

Two days after the Braves beat the Yankees in the World Series, the Dodgers announced that they were leaving Brooklyn and moving to Los Angeles in 1958. A sportswriter asked Roy if he intended to move with them or, in view of his physical condition, stay in New York and perhaps retire from baseball.

"Are you kidding, man?" Roy exclaimed. "I said it before and I'll say it again. The only way they're gonna get this uniform off me is to cut it off."

Which, almost literally, they finally were forced to do.

Not very many weeks later, on a raw January night, he left his store in Harlem and began driving home to Long Island. On a slippery S-curve, about a mile from home, he lost control of his car as the wheels skidded on a patch of ice. The car careened off the road, smashed into a telephone pole.

The accident left him partially paralyzed, confined to a wheelchair for the rest of his life.

In tribute to him, the Dodgers retired his number. No player on that team would ever wear number 39 again.

Ever the man of faith, of courage, Roy refused to hide himself away and retire from active life. He fought back, taught himself to get about, regained some of his independence. Before long he was back in business, and returned to his first and everlasting love, baseball, as a television commentator, interviewing outstanding players after Yankee ball games.

As baseball was always so much a part of Roy Campanella, so Roy would always be a part of baseball.

Mickey Cochrane

3

"YES, that's the life," the young Boston University student said to his companion. They were sitting on the steps of one of the university buildings, basking in the warm spring sunshine, looking out across Boylston Avenue's trolley tracks toward the Brunswick Hotel. On the verandah of the hotel a man sat in a cushioned wicker chair, feet propped on the railing, smoking in what was apparently peaceful and luxurious contentment.

"That's Ty Cobb," said his companion, a rangy, black-haired student named Gordon Stanley Cochrane.

"Cobb!" said the first boy. "Wow! It must be great, just traveling around, playing baseball all the time, making good money. . . ." His voice trailed off on a lingering note of envy.

Cochrane, known on the campus as Mickey, nodded his assent. He was tempted, at that moment, to let his friend in on his secret, but thought better of it. For Mickey Cochrane had more than just a spectator's idea of what that life might be like. He had already tasted it, nibbled at the edges, and soon, very soon, he would get to bite off his first big chunk of life as a professional ballplayer.

That spring of 1923, Mickey had been signed by the Dover, Delaware, team of the Eastern Shore League, and when school was out that spring, he would play with the team on a full-time basis.

However, Mickey was confronted by a serious problem. He still had a semester to go at Boston University, where he was a star, all-around athlete. Come autumn he wanted to continue playing varsity football, perhaps continue with the boxing team. This would be out of the question, of course, if he became involved in professional sports, even though it was baseball, and not boxing or football. He had been careful to avoid mixing college baseball with his new professional career until this point, but now he had to make up his mind.

He resolved the conflict by playing for Dover that summer under the name of Frank King. He was shunted around the infield, outfield and caught as well that summer, appearing in sixty-five games and batting .322. Essentially, however, Mickey considered himself a catcher. He didn't like the idea of being used as an all-around utility man. Moreover, he knew that while he could hit anything that was pitched at him, he was not a skilled fielder. In the outfield he was especially bad at judging high fly balls, and in fact led the league in errors that season with thirteen.

The following year, with college behind him, Mickey dropped his assumed name and, as Mickey Cochrane, went to Portland, in the Pacific Coast League.

While he was in Portland, Mickey caught the attention of Tom Turner, a scout for the Philadelphia Athletics. Turner followed him around like a shadow, saw him walloping the best pitching the league could throw

at him, and reported back to the Athletics that the youngster was the hottest prospect in the league.

"Cochrane can't field a ball at any position," Turner
said, "but he hits like a demon. He's a fierce competitor."

The Athletics, led by Connie Mack, were then in the
process of rebuilding the team, spending large amounts
of money for ballplayers—some of it in vain. They had
paid $50,000 in 1923 for Paul Strand, which had turned
out to be a total loss as Strand failed to make the grade.
Another $50,000 bought outfielder Al Simmons and
more than $100,000 was paid for pitcher Lefty Grove.

On scout Turner's recommendation, and manager
Mack's further insistence, club president Thomas Shibe
agreed to try to buy Cochrane. But it wasn't that easy;
Portland was not a Philadelphia franchise, and the Athletics were not the only major league team interested in
the hard-hitting youngster.

Since the Athletics were spending a small fortune on
players anyway, they decided to invest still further. To
make sure they got Cochrane, they bought the Portland
club!

How much exactly Mickey cost the A's is difficult to
assess, but Connie Mack estimated, some seasons later,
that considering how much money they lost with the
Portland franchise, Cochrane cost more than a quarter
of a million dollars. At that, it was a bargain.

At first it appeared to be another Paul Strand disaster, however. In spring training of 1925 Mickey looked
like anything but a major league catcher, for that was
where Mack decided he should play. The A's had Cy
Perkins, a truly fine receiver, but Mack wisely decided
that Mickey was a better hitter than Perkins, and also
was seven years younger.

Mickey looked pathetic in spring training, except
when he stood in the batting cage. He couldn't catch, he
couldn't handle a pop fly, he didn't know what to do with

a bunt. In his two minor league seasons he had appeared in a total of only 164 games, 40 of them as a catcher.

Day after day Mickey took extra fielding practice with Perkins. He literally spent hours trying to catch pop flies, while his veteran mentor stood by, clucking sympathetically as the ball dropped with terrible regularity, untouched or off the end of the mitt.

One day in March, Mack asked Perkins for an assessment of Mickey's progress.

"He's got a lot of guts and spirit," Perkins said. "But I can see where I'll be doing most of the catching again this year." Mack nodded. A team could do a lot worse than have a stylish receiver like Perkins behind the plate. But . . . he wasn't convinced Perkins was right. Cochrane was a fighter all right. Mack liked that, and he knew with the wisdom of his many years in baseball that a man's will could overcome many handicaps. Moreover, the way Cochrane was hitting in spring training, it would be a shame if his bat had to be kept out of the lineup.

Later that spring a much worried Shibe went to Mack with Cochrane on his mind. What he had heard was not altogether to his liking; another disaster like the Strand affair and the stockholders would have his scalp.

"Well, what do you think about Cochrane?" he asked.

Mack smiled. "He doesn't know how to catch and he's no good on foul pops," he said. "But—he can hit, he can run, he can throw, he's a fighter, and he can learn. He's going to be all right."

"Perkins says he'll be doing all the catching again this year," Shibe said.

"I don't think he will," Mack said.

However, on opening day, it was Perkins behind the mask, not Mickey. Despite the baseball instinct that told him Cochrane would be one of the great ones, Mack felt obliged to start the season with the man who had caught more than one hundred games for him each year since 1919.

The immortal Walter Johnson was pitching for the Senators against Philadelpha on that day. As usual, he was superb. Twice in succession he struck out Perkins. In the eighth inning, with a rally going, Perkins came up again. But Mack called him back to the bench. "Cochrane's going to hit," the A's skipper said.

Up came Cochrane for his first major league at-bat, and he promptly blasted one of Johnson's fast balls off the fence for a double. With that one blow he also blasted the veteran Perkins right out of the Athletics' lineup.

The next afternoon, the starting catcher was Mickey Cochrane.

To Perkins' everlasting credit, it must be said that he took his sudden demotion gracefully. In fact, while he could have held Cochrane back by minding his own business, allowing the rookie to stew in the unsavory juices of his own fielding blunders, Perkins took Cochrane under his wing and taught him how to catch.

"You're too high behind the plate," he told Mickey one day. "Fast-ball pitchers like Grove like a catcher down low. They like the idea of throwing down to the catcher, seems to put a little extra on the fast ball."

Mickey tried it, and found that while it was true the pitchers seemed to like the low target, he was out of position to throw to second on the base stealers. He mentioned this problem to Perkins, who told him:

"You're right, but are you catching for the pitcher, or for your own convenience? Sure, the easy way is to catch high, so you're better set for a throw to the bag when a runner goes down. The real trick is to throw out a runner when you're low down, where you should be, and when he's got a good jump on the pitcher. That's the mark of a real pro."

With Perkins showing him the way, Mickey improved quickly and remarkably. He threw himself into the learning of his craft with savage determination and concentration. By the end of the season he was a good, dependable catcher.

His hitting needed little improvement from the beginning. Still he tried to correct what little weaknesses he did demonstrate, the kind most rookies showed, and which were the products of inexperience. Before the 1925 season was many weeks old, even the veteran pitching stars of the league knew Mickey was no ordinary hitter; he murdered the fast balls, the curves, the screwballs and even the spitballs they threw at him. Everything bounced off the walls of the ball parks. In 134 games he caught that freshman season, Mickey batted .331.

He grew in stature each year, catching more than one hundred games each season, completely relegating Perkins to the background. He followed his rookie season with averages of .273 and .338, and then, in 1928, though he fell to .293, won the American League's Most Valuable Player Award. More than anything else, his fantastic drive won that award for him. He played with a relentless intensity, driving his teammates along with him, battling with them when he thought they were letting down, bringing them to the edge of a pennant victory in 1928.

It was an irritating source of frustration to him that the Athletics were chronic near misses. In the 1928 season he had whipped the team into a high point of competition that brought them into the league lead in early September, only to have the Yankees sweep a three-game series and take the pennant by two and a half games.

Mickey's combative spirit was closer to Ty Cobb's than any other player in baseball, and Cobb has always been generally regarded as probably the one greatest ballplayer of all time. When the 1929 season began, observers could feel the tension in Mickey. He was determined to break the spell the Yankees had cast over the entire league for three straight seasons.

Mack had good material to work with that year. The infield, a patchwork affair in 1928, was set with Jimmy Foxx at first base, Max Bishop at second, Joe Boley at shortstop and Jimmy Dykes at third. In the outfield were Al Simmons, Mule Haas and Bing Miller. The mound staff boasted such great names as Lefty Grove, George Earnshaw, Ed Rommel, Howard Ehmke, Jack Quinn and Rube Walberg.

Of course the Yankee lineup was equally impressive —perhaps even more impressive, for the Yankees of that era were the Yankees of Ruth and Gehrig and Meusel.

The season began in customary fashion, with the Yankees jumping off to the lead, the Athletics trailing. Cochrane was furious. He believed that his club was better than the Yankee aggregation, but what they lacked, and what the Yankees had that was of prime importance, was the psychology of the winner. In the first weeks of that 1929 season he sensed a complacency about the Athletics, an acceptance of their standing as a second-place club, doomed to follow forever at the heels of the unbeatable Yankees.

One day early in May, the Athletics were taking a beating in New York, and taking it listlessly. Waite Hoyt was setting them down with ease. It appeared on the bench that the players were just waiting for the game to be over so they could shower and go back to the hotel for a good meal and an evening on the town.

Midway during the game, as the team returned to the bench after the Yankees were retired, Mickey remained standing in front of the dugout. He waited until all the players had settled comfortably in the shade. He stood there in front of them, mask in his hand, still wearing his protective gear, his dark hair falling over his sweat-streaked forehead, his face grimy and red with rage.

"Why you dirty bunch of yellow dogs!" he snarled at them. "Are you gonna quit? You gonna let these guys beat our brains out over and over again and just sit there with your hands folded on your bellies?"

He turned away from them and angrily tore off his catching tools. First to bat in that inning, he strode to the rack, grabbed a bat, stomped up the plate and rapped Waite Hoyt for a double off the right-field wall. Simmons, batting behind him in the clean-up spot, singled him home. Foxx followed with a home run. Miller singled. Hoyt was taken out, but Dykes greeted reliefer Tom Zachary with a double.

Shamed and inspired, the Athletics beat the Yankees that afternoon, and the next afternoon, and before the month was out they had taken over the league lead.

It wasn't all smooth sailing the rest of the way. The Athletics held onto the lead tenaciously, but the Yankees weren't easily beaten. Every game between the two clubs was fought savagely; neither team could afford to let up for a moment. Mickey was tireless in his efforts to keep the team spirit alive, to keep them fighting.

Once, at home in Shibe Park, pitcher Rube Walberg began to weaken in the late innings of a close contest. The Athletics held a 2–1 lead over the Yankees, going into the eighth inning. With one out, Walberg walked Ruth and Gehrig followed with a single.

Mickey called time and walked slowly out to the mound. Walberg stood there, visibly tired.

Mickey looked at him. "You know what you remind me of?" he said to Walberg.

"What?" the pitcher asked.

"You remind me more of a gutless, washed-up old bum than a major league pitcher." With that Mickey turned on his heel and walked back behind the plate.

Fuming with rage, Walberg reached back for his last

reserve of strength. He struck out Bob Meusal and got Tony Lazzeri on a pop fly to Dykes.

In the ninth he set the Yankees down without a ball being hit out of the infield. The Athletics widened their league lead by another game. It was a week before Walberg would even so much as nod to Mickey off the ball field, but the catcher had gotten the message home and the game won, which was what mattered to him.

Driven by this kind of fiery spirit, and with six regulars batting better than .300, the Athletics broke the Yankees' three-year grip on the pennant with a vengeance. They won by 18 games. Mickey hit .331, batted in 95 runs, and led the league's catchers in put-outs and fielding percentage.

The Athletics faced a formidable foe in the World Series—the Chicago Cubs, led by Joe McCarthy, later to become one of the most successful of New York Yankee managers. McCarthy's 1929 Chicago club had a powerful array of sluggers: Rogers Hornsby, Kiki Cuyler, Hack Wilson and Charley Grimm. Charley Root, Guy Bush and Pat Malone were the pitching aces who helped Chicago win the National League flag by ten and a half games.

Everybody in baseball expected Connie Mack to start Lefty Grove for the Series opener. Only three people knew, and had known two weeks before the Series began, that Grove would not start. With a bit of backstage maneuvering, Mack and Mickey Cochrane decided to spring a surprise. Howard Ehmke would start in the first game. Ehmke had been nursing a sore arm all season, had pitched only fifty-five innings, won seven and lost two. And he was thirty-six years old.

Still, four of his victories were over the Yankees, and in his last outing he had shut out the White Sox. Exactly why Mack chose Ehmke even the wily manager himself wasn't sure; it was one of those unaccountable urges of instinct that turn out to be strokes of genius. In any case, Mack discussed his idea with Cochrane, who told him, "Howard will beat 'em. He's got the guts, and I'll climb all over his back if he starts to let down."

During the final two weeks of the season, Mack sent Ehmke around to scout the Cubs secretly. He felt there would be an important psychological advantage to presenting the Cubs, suddenly, with a pitcher supposedly troubled with a sore arm, when they were expecting a master like Grove. They would figure, "What is Mack up to? What does Ehmke suddenly have that he gets the call to open the World Series instead of Grove or Earnshaw?"

The surprise was complete indeed. The Cubs, the Athletics themselves, and the more than fifty thousand fans who attended the opener in Chicago were stunned when they saw Ehmke warming up and the loudspeaker announced him as the starting pitcher.

All were perhaps even more stunned when Ehmke began pitching like a strong-armed youngster against the powerful Cubs. The game old veteran was putting everything he had into every pitch, wanting desperately to justify the faith Mack was showing. For six innings he and Charley Root dueled without a score. As good as Root was, Ehmke was even better, rolling up a long list of strikeouts.

In the seventh Foxx homered, and the A's had a 1–0 lead. Ehmke was beginning to feel the cold Chicago winds stiffening his arm, but he toiled on courageously, Mickey chattering away constantly, calling encouragement with each pitch, aware that his pitcher was tiring, the old arm stiffening. At the end of eight innings, Ehmke had twelve strikeouts, tying the World Series record set by Ed Walsh in 1906.

As Mickey came to bat in the top of the ninth inning, he had Ehmke weighing heavily on his mind. That one-run margin was an extra strain on the old hurler's nerves, he thought. Runs, insurance runs, that's what Ehmke and the Athletics needed.

He stepped up to the plate, facing relief pitcher Guy Bush. He let a strike go by, fouled off another pitch, ran the count to two balls and two strikes, then lined a single to right field. Simmons followed with another single, and as Mickey came barreling into third, Simmons took second on the throw to third baseman Bub McMillan.

Bing Miller sent both men home with a single, and the Athletics now had a 3–0 lead.

With that three-run cushion, Mickey relaxed a bit. Unfortunately so did Ehmke. He got Wilson out to begin the last half of the ninth, but then Cuyler hit a smash to third. Dykes stopped the hard-hit ball, but threw wildly to first and Cuyler wound up on second. Jackson "Old Hoss" Stephenson, a .362 hitter for Chicago that year, belted a single and the Cubs had a run. Grimm singled, and now the tying runs were on the base paths. Footsie Blair came up to pinch-hit for catcher Mike Gonzalez and hit to Dykes, who threw for the force on Grimm.

Two out, two men still on. Chick Tolson came up to hit for pitcher Bush. Ehmke, working him carefully, ran the count to two balls and two strikes. Cochrane signaled for a fast ball. Ehmke whistled one in, but outside for ball three. A walk would load the bases, put two runs in scoring position. Tolson, a utility first baseman, was not a great hitter (.257 that year) but considered to be a cool two-strike hitter.

Cochrane called time and went to the mound. He huddled with Ehmke for a few moments, then returned and crouched behind the plate. Instead of giving the signal, however, he began talking to Tolson. Nervously, Tolson began to fidget as Mickey chatted away.

Umpire Bill Klem became restive. "Play ball, Cochrane!" he snapped.

Mickey hung out the sign, but as agreed at the mound strategy conference, Ehmke shook him off. And shook him off again, as Tolson became increasingly fidgety. Finally, after another shake-off, Ehmke nodded and delivered a sweeping curve. As the pitcher let go, Mickey yelled, "Hit it!"

Tolson swung—and missed by a foot.

Mickey jumped up jubilantly, waving the ball in his fist. The Athletics had taken the Series opener, 3–1, Ehmke not only had his victory, which turned out to be the last one of his career, but also had set a new World Series record with his thirteenth strikeout of the game.

The Athletics took the second game, 9–3, behind Earnshaw, with Mickey contributing a single, a walk and scoring two runs. In the third game he broke a scoreless deadlock in the fifth inning, reaching Guy Bush for a single to start the rally. Simmons sacrificed, then Bing Miller sent him home with another single. But the Cubs came back for three runs in the sixth to win, 3–1.

The next day the big Cub hitters really went to work. They clobbered Jack Quinn, Rube Walberg and Eddie Rommel, and after six and a half innings had an 8–0 lead, with ace Charley Root coasting along. He had given up only three hits in six innings, two of them a single and double by Cochrane.

Al Simmons opened the Athletics' seventh with a home run. Foxx singled. Then Miller, Dykes and Boley singled. Suddenly the A's had three runs. George Burns hit for Rommel and popped out, but Bishop singled for the fourth run of the inning. Now the fans began to sit up and take notice. What had at first seemed like a harmless rally was assuming the proportions of a real threat to the Cubs' big lead.

Art Nehf replaced Root on the mound. Mule Haas

greeted him with a long blast to center field. Hack Wilson chased it, got the range on it, then suddenly was blinded by the sun and lost it. The ball flew by him and bounced all the way to the center-field wall. Haas legged it around the bases for an inside-the-park home run, scoring behind Boley and Bishop. The score was now 8–7, and the fans in Connie Mack Stadium were going wild.

Mickey came up next and coaxed Nehf for a walk. Out came Nehf, in came Sheriff Blake. Simmons singled, Mickey charging around to third. Foxx singled, and Mickey scored the tying run. Out came Blake, in came Pat Malone, who promptly hit Bing Miller with a pitch, loading the bases. Dykes doubled for two more runs before Malone retired the side.

Ten runs came across the plate in that memorable seventh inning, the greatest single-inning scoring production in World Series history. Grove came on and nailed down the victory, retiring all six men he faced, four of them on strikeouts.

The momentum of that stirring rally carried the Athletics through to the World Championship, clinching the title with a 3–2 victory next day behind Ehmke and Walberg.

Dykes was the slugging hero of the Series, with a .421 average. Right behind him was Mickey, with .400.

He seemed to be sitting on top of the world, playing at his peak, regarded as the best catcher in baseball. But Mickey had financial problems. The famous stock market crash of 1929 had taken all his money, for he, like many ballplayers, had invested heavily in the market. Instead of brooding, however, Mickey decided to become an even more invaluable player, so he could command higher salaries.

Accordingly, in 1930 he drove himself to new heights, hitting a career batting peak of .357, again leading the Athletics to a pennant. Then he hit two home runs in the World Series against the Cardinals as the A's retained the World Championship.

The stock market crash had a much more profound effect on his career, however, than simply improving his batting average. In the depression that followed, the Athletics began losing money. The ball parks were empty. Few people had money to spend on baseball games. Connie Mack and his associates began selling their stars to raise cash. Another pennant in 1931 didn't help their financial position, and when the Yankees beat them out of the pennant in 1932, the A's sold Simmons, Dykes and Haas.

The break-up was completed the following season, after the team finished third. Grove was sold to the Red Sox, and Mickey to the Tigers. Frank Navin, the Detroit owner, paid $100,000 for Mickey, and at once named him as manager of the Bengals.

The change in Detroit fortunes was immediate and spectacular. Mickey was a popular but tough leader. He inspired the Tiger players, who had become immobilized after years of second-division finishes. He drove them mercilessly, but he drove himself no less, and the players respected him.

The change was evident from opening day of the 1934 season. The Tigers were in the thick of the pennant race, led by the slugging of Cochrane, Charley Gehringer, their great second baseman, and home run king Hank Greenberg, the first baseman. For first-line pitchers Mickey had Schoolboy Rowe, Eldon Auker and Tommy Bridges.

The pennant battle was a tough one. The Tigers were in a constant turmoil with the Yankees and the Indians. Mickey found that while his fiery temperament was suited for both playing and managing, the combination of responsibilities was driving him to exhaustion. He seemed to be operating in a constant near rage, ready to burst open at the slightest provocation. "Black Mike" they called him around the league.

In September the Tigers finally broke away, smashed the Yankees in a doubleheader, and went on to win the pennant by five games. Mickey hit .320, with 76 runs batted in. He was regarded as the miracle man of the year, bringing the second division Tigers to a pennant in his first season as manager. And though he failed to win the World Series, losing to the Cardinals, later that autumn, Mickey received the reward he so richly deserved. The Baseball Writers Association of America, which had begun bestowing the award in 1931, named him the Most Valuable Player in the American League.

Some said it was the beating the Tigers took from the Cardinals in the 1934 World Series; others said they were never that good in the first place, the pennant was a fluke. Either way, the team couldn't get going early in 1935. They were in last place for the first month. Cochrane drove himself insanely, trying to rally them. He became a ghostly figure, thin and drawn, a bundle of nerves. He was too weak to throw and to hit.

Cy Perkins, the veteran receiver who had helped him, and whom he had beaten out for the Athletics' job, was now one of his coaches. Perkins tried to shake him out of his suicidal drive. "You're killing yourself, Mickey," he said to him one day, "and you're killing the team, too. You can't be all over the place at once. You gotta take it a little easy. If you don't snap out of it we're all sunk."

Cochrane heeded the words of his old friend and mentor. Without in any way lessening his drive, he forced himself to direct his energies toward catching and team strategy. Losing a game did not throw him into a fit of black depression, from which he used to rouse himself only by a fresh frenzy of activity. He still hated to lose, but at least he could accept defeat.

Gradually he worked his way out of his deep batting slump. He went from below .200 to a season of .319, but he caught only 115 games, his lowest mark since he broke into the major leagues. Still, he managed the Tigers into their second straight pennant.

This time the Cubs were their opponents. Led by manager Charley Grimm, the Cubs of 1935 had such stalwart sluggers as Gabby Hartnett, Mickey's arch rival for catching honors, Augie Galan, Stan Hack and Phil Cavarretta. Charley Root was still one of their top hurlers, aided by Lon Warneke, Larry French and Tex Carleton.

The Cubs took the first game, then Detroit the next three. On the brink of extinction, the Cubs came back to win the fifth game, beating Rowe, 3–1.

It was Bridges against French in the sixth game. Both pitchers were hit hard in the opening innings, and the score was 3–3 going into the last half of the ninth at Detroit. Mickey had accounted for one of the runs, scoring after opening a rally with a single. Now, with one out, he rapped French for his second single of the game. Gehringer grounded to first, and Mickey took second on the play.

Two out, and up came Goose Goslin. He cracked a single to left. Mickey took off for third and rounded the bag. Though the ball was hit sharply to left, Mickey felt he could beat Galan's throw. He barreled down the line as Hartnett stood there, waiting for the throw. In came Mickey, in came the throw from Galan—but too late! Cochrane was home with the winning run, the run that brought Detroit the first World Series title in its entire history.

Mickey was mobbed by his teammates as he crossed the plate. He was not only a hero to them, but a hero to all of Detroit. He could have been elected mayor. Two seasons as manager, and he had brought a second-division team to two straight pennants and its first World Championship.

Mickey could have rested on his accomplishments of those two years. He was thirty-three years old, and the years of driving himself ruthlessly were beginning to leave marks. Though his hands were remarkably free of damage, his legs were weary and bruised. Moreover, he was emotionally exhausted.

He wanted to establish an American League dynasty in Detroit, wanted the Tigers to win every pennant as long as he was their manager and their catcher. At the very least, he wanted to make it three straight pennants, to match the three straight he had helped bring home to Philadelphia. He had to battle the Yankees again in 1936, but they were too tough for him. Mickey again drove himself to the limit—and, finally, over the limit. He suffered a complete nervous breakdown. Without him, the Tigers finished second.

He came back in 1937 with renewed vigor, opening the season like the Cochrane of old, driving, inspiring the team in its now annual struggle with the Yankees. On May 25 the Bengals were at the Stadium, and in the third inning Mickey hit his second homer of the young season to tie the score.

He came up again in the fifth with two out and outfielder Pete Fox on first. Bump Hadley was on the mound for the Yankees. He pitched carefully to Cochrane. The count went to three balls and one strike. Then a fast ball, high inside, came buzzing up to the plate. Mickey began to draw back, then it appeared as though he lost sight of the ball momentarily. It struck him in the side of the head with a terrible thud.

Mickey went down as though struck by a bullet, unconscious. He was rushed to the hospital, where an examination revealed a triple fracture of the skull. For days Mickey lingered near death. But from the darkness of his coma the fighting spirit of Mickey Cochrane rallied the forces of his body, and he recovered.

To no one's surprise, he appeared at the ball park one day, ready to don the catching tools and go back to work. Walter Briggs, the club president, ordered him back to the dugout. "No more catching for you, Mickey," he said. "We need you healthy, to manage this club."

Reluctantly, Mickey remained on the bench, directing the Tigers to another second-place finish.

Bench manager was not his idea of baseball, however. He couldn't sit still while the action was going on, particularly if the club was doing badly. He came near suffering another nervous breakdown in 1938 when the Tigers couldn't get out of the second division, and he could do nothing but pace in front of the dugout like the caged Tiger that he was.

He didn't last out the season. He was fired.

Physically and emotionally spent, Mickey retired. In 1947, he was voted into baseball's Hall of Fame as one of the all-time catching greats of the game, with a lifetime batting average of .320.

In 1950, after eleven years away from baseball, he was called back by the man who called him in the beginning of it all—Connie Mack. In the golden anniversary of his managing career, Mack hired two of his old cronies to coach for him, Mickey and Bing Miller. During the season, Mickey was promoted to general manager of the club, but a dispute arose when Mack's two sons took over in September, and Mickey resigned.

He returned once again, however, for baseball was always very much in his blood. In 1955 he became a scout for the Yankees, then a scout and instructor for the Tigers, ending his baseball life where he had spent his two most glorious years.

When measuring the talents of such as Cochrane, Dickey, Hartnett, Campanella and Berra, it is difficult to separate, evaluate and find an order of greatness. However, no catcher, no player in fact, ever had more fighting spirit, more competitive drive, than "Black Mike" Cochrane.

4

IT occurred suddenly to William Malcolm Dickey that he was a tired man. Thirty-six years old, he had just completed his sixteenth year in the major leagues, sixteen years with the great New York Yankees. He had shown them a thing or two this past season, though, creaking bones or no, catching 85 games and hitting .351, the second best average of his life. Now he was going into his ninth World Series, and he hoped that there, too, he could carve out some special memory for himself.

This would be, after all, his last World Series. His last appearance in baseball as well. He was convinced of that. When the World Series was over he was taking his thirty-six years into the United States Navy. There was a desperate war on, that year of 1943, and it was time for him to contribute what he could, in any way they asked. And when it was all over, it was hardly likely he would be in a position to put on the old tools and squat behind the plate. Still, he'd had his years, and he had no complaints.

Bill Dickey was born into baseball. His father, who worked for the Missouri and Pacific Railroad, had once pitched and caught for Memphis. Later, when John Dickey moved the family to Kensett, Arkansas, where the railroad transferred him, he starred with the local semi-pro baseball team. It would have been surprising if the three young Dickey boys had not hungered for a career in baseball.

While Bill and his kid brother George—they called him Skeets—were out playing ball on the sandlots of Kensett, big brother Gus was already making a name for himself as a second baseman and pitcher in the East Arkansas semipro league. Bill, too, fancied himself a pitcher, while Skeets wanted to be a catcher. However, the family talents were so varied that each of the boys could play at several positions.

"Best not to get too set in one position till you find out what you do the most natural," John Dickey told his sons. He had high hopes that one, at least, would make the major leagues, and he worked and drilled them constantly, instilling in them a tremendous desire for continous improvement, for the goal of near perfection.

"A professional athlete can't stay in the same place," he advised them. "If he doesn't try to get a little bit better all the time, then he'll get a little bit worse."

Unhappily for Gus, a truly talented player, he hurt his arm while playing in the East Arkansas League, and had to quit baseball. That left it to Bill and Skeets, who were still in school.

Bill's versatility paid off while he was in high school. He couldn't play baseball for the school team, because the high school was four miles away from his home, in another town, actually, and he couldn't manage the time schedule. However, the Kensett town nine needed a second baseman. Gus had played second, and had taught Bill the basics of work around the bag. Bill won the

102

job, and was the Sunday star second baseman for Kensett.

"Better than I ever was at second," Gus used to boast proudly about his kid brother.

Happy enough to play, Bill didn't complain, though second base was not his favorite spot. He still longed to either pitch or catch. When he got to Little Rock College, he found his chance.

He tried out for the Little Rock team as a pitcher, and made it. Little Rock already had a top pitcher, however, named Jimmy Froley. What the team needed was a good catcher to work with Froley. The two men joined forces. When Froley pitched, Bill caught. Bill would then pitch the next game, and Froley would catch him. They became a tremendously successful one-two combination for Little Rock College, and good friends as well.

Froley, who was older, used to catch on Sundays for a semipro team in Hot Springs, Arkansas. One day in the spring of 1925 Froley asked his friend for a favor.

"Bill," he began, "how about taking over for me at Hot Springs next Sunday?"

Bill wasn't too enthusiastic about the idea. "Tell you the truth, Jimmy," he replied, "it doesn't pay enough money just to go over to Hot Springs for the day."

"I know," Froley said. "But I got a chance to play next Sunday with another team, for more money, and I'd sure like the chance. If you don't sub for me, I can't go."

Bill finally agreed, reluctantly. He found, when he arrived in Hot Springs, that manager Roy Gillenwater wasn't any happier to see him than he was to be there. But he needed a catcher, and he let Bill put on the tools.

Pitching that afternoon for Hot Springs was the team's star hurler, Spike Hunter, who later got as far as a brief try with the Athletics. An experienced semipro in the summer of 1925, he was a bit dubious about the talents of this college kid. He soon changed his mind.

Bill set to work confidently, calling the signals as though he had worked a dozen times with Hunter. The Hot Springs team won. Hunter was impressed. So was manager Gillenwater.

Jimmy Froley never did get his job back.

The Hot Springs club was a good semipro team, attracting major league scouts regularly. In particular there was a hard-hitting outfielder named Paul Phillips on the club, a youngster Gillenwater touted as true professional material. He tipped off Lena Blackburne, who managed the Little Rock Travelers, of the Southern Association. Late in July, Blackburne came down for a look at Phillips, bringing with him club owner Bob Allen.

After six innings, Allen said to his skipper, "Well, what do you think of Phillips?"

"Never mind Phillips," Blackburne said, "I want that kid catcher. He's got an arm like a rifle."

"Well, go get him, then," Allen said.

After the game Blackburne went down to see Bill, told him who he was, and said he would like him to sign then and there to play for Little Rock.

Bill was thunderstruck. He was aware enough of baseball's workings to realize that scouts were always around, watching the colleges, the sandlots, the semipros, always searching for young talent. But it hadn't occurred to him that anybody was at this game, or that it was possible to be signed and thus become a pro just like that.

Of course, he jumped at the chance. He didn't even ask what the salary might be. As for Blackburne, he suddenly realized he had no contract forms with him, not even a scrap of paper. He thought for a moment of coming back the following week with formal papers, but decided that course was dangerous. The area was alive with scouts. In fact the owner of the Fort Smith club had also seen this game. In a week somebody else might grab this kid.

While Bill looked on curiously Blackburne searched his pockets, then his wallet. Finally, with a shrug, he removed his membership card in the Elks. It was blank on the reverse side. He scribbled out a short agreement and handed the card to Bill.

"Here, kid," he said, "sign this."

Bill looked at the man in astonishment.

"It's okay, it's okay," Blackburne said. "Later we'll get it down on paper."

It was early August of 1925 when Bill Dickey donned his first professional baseball uniform. There was no bonus involved, not a nickel, and his salary was a small one. It was a deal that by today's standards must be considered one of the greatest bargains of all time.

Blackburne didn't work him much, allowing him to catch batting practice and warming up the bullpen pitchers. He did get into three games, hit three singles in ten trips for a .300 average.

Bill forgot about college now. He never wanted to be anything but a baseball player. Here, apparently, he was getting his chance. He was confident that he would make it all the way. When he reported to Little Rock in the spring of 1926 a new manager had taken over. Joe Cantillion had a proud reputation as a handler and judge of young players. He saw at once that Dickey had unlimited potential, but needed seasoning. Little Rock was too high a league for him. He would have to sit on the bench here, where more experienced catchers were working.

Accordingly, Cantillion tried to waive him to Muskogee, down a notch in the minor league standings. But if the Little Rock manager didn't think Dickey had the stuff yet, the other Southern Association clubs dis-

105

agreed. They refused to let Dickey pass. By baseball rules, a team couldn't send a player to a lesser league without first offering him to all the other teams in the league. If no team picked up this option, the player could be sent down. If any team claimed him, as it were, "on waivers," at the league's set waiver price, the original club had the right to withdraw its offer.

Cantillion was disturbed. "The kid needs work," he said to his aides, "and he won't get it here. We got to figure out a way."

They found a way, using the complicated workings of organized baseball to their advantage this time. Instead of sending Dickey down, Cantillion sent him up—to Minneapolis of the American Association. Of course, the promotion required no prior waivers from the other teams.

Then Minneapolis sent him to Muskogee. The other American Association teams readily waived the untried youngster out of their high minor league. The maneuvers were all quite bewildering to Bill, who actually remained immobile during the complicated process. The arrangements all were done on paper.

In the Western Association, Dickey quickly found himself put to the test. It was a running league, and base runners wasted no time trying to run a rookie right out of baseball. To their chagrin, they found themselves being cut down regularly by Dickey's rifle throws. In sixty-one games he made fifty-eight assists.

It was this defensive skill, more than batting prowess, that hustled Bill right back to Little Rock. He hit well enough at Muskogee—.283, with seven homers—but his work behind the plate convinced Cantillion he was ready, and he brought him up. Strangely enough, despite the improvement in pitching he faced, Bill walloped the ball there at a .391 clip while catching twenty-one games.

For an inexperienced eighteen-year-old, it had been quite a season.

He was, then, a chattel of the Chicago White Sox, who owned the Little Rock franchise. Normally, he would have gone up the chain to Chicago. That strange tangled web of baseball law caught up with him again, however, affecting the history of American League baseball for nearly twenty years. The White Sox slipped up somewhere, failing to exercise a necessary option. Following the season at Muskogee and Little Rock, they sent him to Jackson, Mississippi, in the Cotton State League. As the number-one receiver there he hit .297, catching 101 games. Again his defensive skill classed him as a future superstar; he led the league in assists, throwing out 84 base runners, in put-outs, with 457, and in fielding average, with .984. He had just nine errors for the season.

During the season the White Sox had been mentally rubbing their hands in anticipation of bringing him up in another season or so, while the scouts of other major league teams watched him and regretted their inability to touch him.

Johnny Nee of the Yankees was one scout who took nothing for granted, however, which was why he was so largely responsible for the building of the awesome Yankee teams of that era. He took a look at Dickey and was convinced at once that this was exceptional material.

He wired the Yankees: "I'll quit scouting if this boy doesn't make good."

The Yankees' formidable machinery went to work. Front office executives discovered that instead of being tied to Chicago, as everyone thought, Dickey was on the open market. Without hesitation they bought him, before anybody else knew negotiations were going on. Though a Chicago franchise, Little Rock had originally bought

Dickey, and so they could sell him to whom they chose, once options had been lost by the parent club.

It was agreed that Bill would start the 1928 season back at Little Rock. This was fine with Bill. He was overwhelmed at his good fortune, but could afford to bide his time. The Yankees of that era were the Yankees of Ruth and Gehrig at their peaks. The 1927 team was the best of its time, smashing the powerful Pirates four straight in the World Series. They had two good catchers in Benny Bengough and Pat Collins. Still, Bill knew that the Yankees had gone to considerable trouble to buy him. When the time was ripe, they would send for him.

The call came sooner than he expected. After hitting .300 for the first half of the season at Little Rock, he was sent upward to Buffalo. No sooner had he arrived there, however, than the Yankees ordered him to report to New York.

It was quite a thrill for the twenty-one-year-old boy from Arkansas to take his place in the locker room alongside Ruth and Gehrig, and Bob Meusel, Tony Lazzeri and Waite Hoyt, and alongside a spirited rookie infielder named Leo Durocher.

The Yankees were too deeply involved in a pennant battle with the Athletics for manager Miller Huggins to throw him directly into action. He did appear in ten games, however, before the season was over, coming in for the final innings to rest either Bengough or Collins.

He sat out the World Series as the Yankees made it eight straight victories, this time sweeping the Cardinals in four games. This awesome display of power had a profound effect on the youngster. It gave him a championship bearing, the psychology of the winner, important assets for any young athlete to own.

There was no awkward period of breaking into the lineup for Dickey. In spring training of the 1929 season manager Huggins felt that the young receiver was ready to take over, and he handed him the catching tools.

"You're my catcher until you prove you're not," he said.

Bill took over eagerly, confident he could handle the job, and at once demonstrated that he could indeed. He hit the toughest American League hurlers with the ease of the naturally great hitter, cut down base runners with such skill that he wound up leading the league in assists with 95. His final batting average of .324 included 10 homers and 65 runs batted in.

Naturally, he had no "book" on the hitters, but he had enough experience and talent to handle such crafty veterans as Waite Hoyt, Herb Pennock and Wilcey Moore with no complaints. The pitchers knew the hitters, and before the season was over they taught Bill most of what he would need to know about them. Veteran hurlers are usually a bit nervous about rookie catchers, but the Yankee mound staff recognized in the new kid receiver a potential superstar.

Despite the addition of Dickey and such fabled stars as Ruth and Gehrig, the Yankees were victims of Connie Mack's great Philadelphia Athletic teams for three straight years. While Dickey was batting .339 in 1930 and .327 in 1931, the Athletics continued to rule the league. It wasn't until 1932, the second year of manager Joe McCarthy's reign, that the New Yorkers managed to break the Atheltics' streak.

The Yankees faced the Chicago Cubs in that 1932 World Series, and dueling against each other as well were Dickey and the Cubs' great Gabby Hartnett. A further flag of battle was raised by manager McCarthy himself, who had been fired by the Cubs in the final week of the 1930 season. Thus there were rivalries on several levels, with the Yankees, proud of their championship history, particularly anxious to restore their crown after an absence of three years.

The Chicago club, under "Jolly Cholly" Grimm, was buried in the first game, 12–6, Dickey batting in two of the runs himself. He did as well in the second contest, getting two singles, and batting in two runs again as Lefty Gomez beat Lon Warneke, 5–2. On the third day Pennock beat Charley Root, 7–5, then the Yankees made it four straight with a 13–6 rout, Bill going three-for-six in the clincher.

With seven hits in the four games, Bill's .438 average was topped only by Gehrig's nine hits and .529 average. Hartnett had five hits and a .313 average. The Yankees regained the World Championship, McCarthy had the last laugh on his former employers, and Bill Dickey was generally regarded now as the best catcher in baseball.

The Yankees' regained crown was soon lost again, however. Nearing forty, the mighty Ruth began to lose his touch, and in fact played just two more seasons with the Yankees. First Washington, then Detroit overcame the weakened New Yorkers, who had Gehrig and Dickey for big guns, but no longer the biggest of them all. Ruth's power was sorely missed.

Dickey meanwhile pounded the ball regularly, season after season, and starred behind the plate, as well. From 1933 through 1935, while his team finished runner-up each year, he hit .312, .322 and .279, leading the league in put-outs two of those three years (1933 and 1935).

There was a feeling, in 1936, that the Yankees were flowering again, due to begin a new dynasty. Dickey, in many ways the backbone of the club, saw the nucleus of this powerful team take shape that spring. "We're going to win it all this year," he proclaimed to the sportswriters. "And the big guy who'll do it for us is right out there," he added, pointing to center field.

110

There, jogging easily over the grass, shagging fungoes, was a hawk-nosed rookie from San Francisco named Joe DiMaggio. The great DiMag was not the only newcomer, however, to become part of the awesome 1936 Yankees. There were George "Twinkletoes" Selkirk, Red Rolfe, Johnny Murphy and Jake Powell.

McCarthy's daily lineup soon became the scourge of the American League. Frankie Crosetti, the shortstop, was leadoff man, followed by Rolfe at third base, DiMaggio, Gehrig at first, then Dickey, Selkirk playing right field, Powell playing left and Tony Lazzeri at second base. This was a terrifying array for any pitcher to face, while the Yankees' mound staff boasted Red Ruffing, Lefty Gomez, Bump Hadley, Monte Pearson and Murphy, the latter developing into one of the all-time great relief pitchers.

With this lineup the Yankees ran away with the pennant, beating the Tigers by nineteen and a half games! Dickey had the finest season of his career, batting .372 with 22 homers and 107 runs batted in.

In the World Series that followed, the Giants gave them a tough battle, carrying them to six games. But the Yankee power was too much, even for such fabled hurlers as Hal Schumacher, Freddie Fitzsimmons and Carl Hubbell. Two Yankee victories were 13–5 and 18–4 routs, in the former Dickey batting in five runs with a homer and a single.

Year after year the new Yankee juggernaut rolled on, crushing everything in its way. There was no question, each season, of who would win the pennant, just: the Yankeees by how many games. Each year, too, Dickey was up there with the top sluggers, batting in more than one hundred runs four straight seasons, leading the team to successive World Championships.

Facing Hartnett again in the 1938 Series, Dickey once again outhit his National League rival, batting .400

to Gabby's .091. He set the Yankees going in the first game by tying a World Series record. He smacked four straight singles, equaling the mark for hits in one game, scored a run, batted one in, and even stole a base, as the Yankees won, 3–1. Then they took the next three for their third straight championship.

Another Yankee immortal fell by the wayside in 1939; still the steam roller thundered on. Ill with a disease that would soon take his life, Lou Gehrig left the club early in the season. As a man, as a symbol, no one would ever replace him. As a slugging machine, however, the Yankees now had Charlie "King Kong" Keller in the outfield, while Babe Dahlgren took over at first base. There was now Joe Gordon, too, the rookie sensation of 1938, playing second base in place of Lazzeri. The Yankees won again, beating the Red Sox by seventeen games.

A new opponent faced them in the 1939 Series—the Cincinnati Reds. Led by Bill McKechnie, the Reds had won their pennant on the pitching of Buckey Walters, a 27-game winner, and Paul Derringer, who had won 25.

The Yankees beat Walters twice, Derringer once and Gene Thompson once, again winning in four straight games. Dickey smashed two homers in this Series and batted in five runs, including the winning one in the 2–1 opening game victory.

Temporarily halted by the Tigers in 1940, the Yankees came back to win the pennant in 1941, beating the Dodgers in the World Series. The following season, the first one played with the United States deeply involved in World War II, they won the pennant, but lost to the Cardinals in the Series.

Dickey was now thirty-six, the dean of major league catchers, recognized as one of the best the game ever produced. Many said, unequivocally, *the* best. As the 1943 season progressed, with the Yankees apparently on their way to another flag, Dickey felt he must contribute what he could to the war effort, despite his years. He was determined that the end of that season, come what may, he would trade his Yankee uniform for a military one.

He caught eighty-five games, showing the baseball world that thirty-six years old was thirty-six years young for Bill Dickey by batting .351.

Again the Yankees faced the Cardinals. Thirsting for revenge, they beat Max Lanier, 4–2, in the first game. Mort Cooper had the Cardinals out front, 4–1, going into the bottom of the ninth, when the Yankees started a rally. Two runs scored, a man was on third. Up came Dickey. He smashed a low line drive past Cooper—it looked like a hit—but second baseman Chuck Klein grabbed the ball, robbing him. Cooper got out of further trouble, and the Cardinals won, 4–3.

Hank Borowy beat Alpha Brazle, 6–2, in the third contest, Bill chipping in with two singles. Then came the fourth contest, Marius Russo against Lanier again. The Yankees led, 2–1, going into the ninth, Dickey's RBI single accounting for one of the runs. With one out, Marty Marion doubled for St. Louis, and Sam Narron came up to pinch-hit for pitcher Harry "The Cat" Brecheen.

Narron was a third-string catcher. The Yankees knew little about him. After a conference on the mound, Dickey decided to have Russo feed him curves. Quickly the Yankee pitcher got two strikes on Narron. Dickey then called for the "waste" pitch, signaling for a fast ball, high outside, setting Narron up for another curve. At the same time, however, he also signaled shortstop Crosetti closer to second, in case Narron bit at the bad pitch and hit it on the ground.

Moving Crosetti was one of the strokes of genius marking a catcher like Dickey. Narron did go for the outside pitch and hit it sharply through the box. Crosetti dashed over, picked up the ball and just nipped Narron at first base. Had he not moved over on Dickey's signal the ball would have gone through for a hit, the game would have been tied, the Cardinals might well have gone on to win and tie the Series.

Instead Russo retired Klein for the final out, locking up the 2–1 victory, giving the Yankees a 3–1 edge.

The Cooper brothers battery faced the Yankees once more in the fifth contest, Mort on the mound, brother Walker behind the plate. For the Yankees, it was Spud Chandler.

Cooper started by striking out the first five Yankees to face him—including Dickey. Chandler, though not as sharp, held the Cardinals scoreless as well. In the bottom of the fifth, with the game still scoreless, Whitey Kurowski led off with a bunt single. Then Chandler walked Ray Sanders on four pitches. Up came Johnny Hopp, and Chandler threw three more balls.

Out to the mound strode Dickey. "You okay?" he asked Chandler.

The pitcher nodded. "I just don't want to give him a clean shot at anything."

"Yeah, but we don't want to fill the bases, either," Dickey said. "There's nobody out, remember. So come on and get the ball over now. No more fooling around."

He went back behind the plate, signaled for a sinker. Chandler threw a strike.

Figuring Hopp had orders to take, Dickey called for a curve. A right-handed pitcher, Chandler threw to the left-handed-hitting Hopp. The ball came right into the plate, just over the knees. Hopp took it for strike two.

Now Dickey called for the fast ball. Chandler threw it outside, but perhaps expecting the pitch to break again, Hopp swung and missed for strike three.

Chandler then got Marty Marion and pitcher Cooper easily to close out the inning.

Cooper meanwhile was still going strong. He retired the first two Yankees to start the sixth, then Keller singled, only the fourth hit for the Yankees, all singles.

Dickey came up next, hoping to keep the rally going. On deck knelt Nick Etten, a hard-hitting first baseman.

Waiting for one of Cooper's fast balls, he got one and caught it. The ball headed toward deep left field. He charged down the line, saw coach Earl Combs wave his fist in the air with glee and thought: This should be good for a run, anyway. He charged around second, headed for third, and then saw that third base coach Art Fletcher was waving his cap around, signaling a home run.

That was all Chandler needed. He settled down, held the Cardinals, and the Yankees won the game and the World Championship, as well as their revenge against the Cardinals.

With one blow, Dickey had done it all. And fittingly, because for all he knew, it would be his last game of baseball. The following spring, before the season began, he went into the Navy as a lieutenant commander.

For two years he roamed the Pacific, a Special Services officer, organizing sports activities in the Navy's remote outposts.

When the war was over and he took off his Navy uniform, Dickey was thirty-nine. But the Yankees wanted him back. There was a new regime at the Stadium. A new owner, Larry McPhail, had bought the Yankees. McPhail didn't work well with manager McCarthy, and the Yankee skipper, in ill health, resigned in May. McPhail asked Dickey to step in as manager. Bill wasn't quite sure he was cut out to be a manager, but he did relish the challenge. He accepted.

Soon he discovered that he didn't get along with McPhail, either. In September he asked to be replaced.

Johnny Neun then became interim manager, though Dickey did finish out the season behind the plate as the Yankees came in third. At thirty-nine, he still was able to catch eighty-five games and hit .261.

In his seventeen seasons with the Yankees, Dickey caught 1,789 games, compiling a lifetime batting average of .313. He holds the major league catching record of one hundred or more games caught per season with thirteen —and they were thirteen straight years, from 1929-1941.

Dickey went home to Little Rock in 1947, managed the minor league team there, even played eight games and batted .333. But his association, his value to the Yankees was not yet ended. In 1949 Casey Stengel took over as manager of the Yankees, and immediately sent for him. The Yankees needed his help. More specifically, there was a strong-hitting, weak-fielding catcher named Lawrence Peter "Yogi" Berra who needed his help.

Dickey remembered Berra vaguely, as a rather likable, awkward kid who had come up to the Yankees in the final days of the 1946 season. Dickey took over as his coach, and turned him into a great receiver. Only when that job was done to his satisfaction did Dickey retire.

In 1954, Bill Dickey was voted into baseball's Hall of Fame.

As veteran sportswriter Dan Daniel said of him, when he went off to war in 1944: "Dickey isn't just a player. He's a ball club."

Gabby Hartnett

5

STAND a ten-year-old American boy up in a classroom and ask him what he wants to be when he grows up. The answers will vary tremendously, of course, but there will always be the standards. Certainly many a ten-year-old boy will say, "A baseball player." A few even realize that childhood ambition. Conversely, many a major league baseball player gave little thought to becoming one, even as he scampered around the sandlots playing the game.

It is quite likely, however, that no Hall of Fame immortal like Charles Leo "Gabby" Hartnett ever had a childhood ambition so bizarrely far afield from baseball. Charles Leo Hartnett, ten years old, one of fourteen children of a New England streetcar conductor, told everybody in town he wanted to become the champion berry picker of all America.

It was understandable, to those who knew the boy's circumstances. With fourteen mouths to feed, Mr. Hartnett senior had little money left over for such simple children's necessities as Saturday afternoon movies and candy bars. So Charles Leo Hartnett went berry picking around the town of Millville, Massachusetts, packed them in quart jars, and sold them for fifteen cents a quart. In that year of 1910, this was a profitable little business for a ten-year-old.

Baseball? A fun game, and little Charles played it. But he didn't regard it seriously. How could a ten-year-old boy make movie money playing baseball? There was no future in the game. Not as a spare-time proposition, at least.

Not too many years later, however, ever industrious Charles Leo Hartnett saw that money could be made from baseball as a sideline. One of his older brothers (there were seven boys, seven girls in the family) played on weekends with an industrial team, and was doing all right. Anything his brother could do, he could do. The company he worked for, makers of rubber boots, had a baseball team, and he became the club's catcher. Catching wasn't his favorite position, but then it wasn't anybody's, so it was the easiest to get.

He was a big, skinny, red-faced lad of nineteen then, strong from many months of work in a wire mill and the rubber factory. He wasn't much behind the plate, but he had courage, and he could hit the ball a mile. He had done precisely that—hit two homers in a twilight game after work one day—when a man who introduced himself as Mr. Mack asked him if he'd like to play professional baseball.

"Would I!" said Charles. "But for who?"

"For me," the man said. "I own the Worcester club. We're in the Eastern League. If you're interested, let's get together."

That's how Charles Leo Hartnett became a professional baseball player. He was no ball of fire at Worcester,

120

hitting .264, but he had something about his style of play that marked him as a future star. At least, it seemed so in the discerning eye of Jack Doyle, a scout for the Chicago Cubs.

Doyle was in the stands one afternoon, watching Worcester play Albany. He had come for no particular reason, to see no special player. New England happened to be the area he covered, and he left no stone unturned, no bush unbeaten in his search for new talent. He had never heard of Charles Leo Hartnett. He saw something that day, however, that gave him the urge to know the young catcher for Worcester a lot better.

It wasn't the way the boy hit the ball, which was impressive but not spectacular. What caught Doyle's practiced eye was a play at the plate. Midway through the game an Albany runner came charging home on a base hit. Hartnett took the throw at the plate. The runner slammed into him full speed, knocking off his hat, sending his mitt flying, almost cutting off his shin guards with flashing spikes. Hartnett was knocked off his feet, but he made the tag and came up holding the ball for the out.

After the game Doyle went around to see Mack, the club owner.

"Who's the red-faced kid you got for catcher?" he asked.

Mack knew Doyle well. "Name's Hartnett," he said. "Picked him up playing industrial ball."

"I like his spirit," Doyle said. "I'll take him."

They shook hands on the deal. Doyle said he would get in touch with the club in Chicago and report back with the details of the sale. A few moments later Hartnett walked into Mack's office and asked to borrow a few dollars against his salary. Mack handed him a five-dollar bill. "Here," he said, "you can pay me back when you get to Chicago."

"Chicago?" Hartnett furrowed his brow. "We don't play in Chicago."

Mack smiled. "You do. The Cubs bought you, just five minutes ago. Next year you play in Chicago."

From industrial baseball to the major leagues in one year was a bit much for the youngster from New England. He wasn't quite prepared psychologically for the rarefied atmosphere of the major leagues, not sure of his capabilities nor of the proper manner of conducting himself in the company of other players and newspapermen.

He met the rest of the team and the rookie hopefuls in Chicago the following year, and then the Cubs went to Catalina Island, off the California coast, for spring training. On the train ride from Chicago to the West Coast he sat quietly in the club car while around him the players and the newspapermen chatted amiably or played cards. The scene, a typical one, was like nothing Hartnett had ever seen before, and he felt, literally, out of his league.

One of the sportswriters, who had been observing his withdrawn silence for some time, suddenly exclaimed loudly, for all in the car to hear, "There's the gabbiest guy that ever went on a spring training trip."

It was nothing but "Gabby" Hartnett forever after.

Gabby almost finished his career with the Cubs before it even got started. Manager Bill Killefer, a former catcher himself, ignored him through the early days of training. When the team went to Los Angeles, later that spring, to begin an exhibition series, Killefer told scout Doyle and John Seys, the traveling secretary, that he was cutting Hartnett from the team.

"But he hasn't even caught a game," Doyle protested. "Why not give the kid a chance?"

Killefer relented. Gabby caught the next afternoon, well enough to fend off the spring-training axe. By the time the exhibition season was over, he had impressed

Killefer enough to win the starting assignment behind the plate on opening day.

With just his one year at Worcester behind him, Gabby's opening day chore was to catch Grover Cleveland Alexander, one of the storied names in baseball's pitching annals. Three times in his career Alexander had won more than thirty games.

Gabby had good reason to be nervous. He had never even seen a major league ball park before. Now, in Crosley Field, Cincinnati, he was giving the signals to old "Pete" Alexander. Before the veteran hurler took the mound, he said to the rookie catcher, "Don't worry about it, kid. Just call your game."

When it was all over, and the Cubs had won, Alexander said to manager Killefer, who had caught him many times, "Bill, the kid's all right."

For the final out of the game Alexander struck out Babe Pinelli, later to become a major league umpire. Gabby held the ball, and the glove he used that day, as souvenirs, the first of many tokens he was to collect later in the course of his colorful career.

It was clear that Gabby had the makings of a fine catcher, indeed a great catcher, but in 1922 he was very much the raw rookie. After the opening day assignment, Killefer relegated him to the bench, and he caught only thirty-one games that year, hitting .194.

The following year Killefer thought it might be a good idea to try him at first base. He put him into a game against Pittsburgh one day. Leading off for the Pirates in the fourth inning was outfielder Max Carey. He topped the ball down the first base line, a slow, twisting roller. Over for it went the pitcher. Down the line came Hartnett, as Carey came charging up from the plate. All four reached the same point at the same time—the pitcher, Carey, Hartnett and the ball. There was a mighty collision; caps and gloves flew in all directions. Gabby made the tag for the out, however. A bit shaken up, he stomped around for a few seconds, getting his wind back, then announced he was ready.

Out from the dugout came Killefer, announcing a new first baseman. "Better sit down before you get killed," the Cubs' pilot said to Gabby. Intermittently throughout the season Killefer tried again, each time with similar, near disastrous results. He decided that if Gabby was going to do anything at all for the Cubs it would have to be as a catcher.

Gabby got the first-string job in 1924, and proved that given that opportunity he could make the grade. He hit .299 that year with 16 homers and 67 runs batted in. He was behind the plate to stay, through record-making years.

It was Gabby's ill luck to come up with a sore arm the first chance he had to play in a World Series. For the first time since he had joined the team the Cubs won the pennant, but early in that 1929 season he developed shoulder trouble that threatened to end his career. His World Series appearances were limited to three hitless trips as a pinch hitter.

There were rumors that he was through, that he wouldn't recover in time for the 1930 season and would be given his release. He proved the pessimists wrong by coming back for the best season of his career. He was a one-man powerhouse, hitting .339 and 37 homers and batting in 122 runs. Despite this tremendous effort, the Cubs finished second to the Cardinals.

They won the pennant in 1932, however, and Gabby finally got to play a full World Series. Unhappily, the Cubs were facing one of the New York Yankees' fabled aggregations, headed by Ruth and Gehrig. Gabby hit .313 for the Series, and hit his first Series homer, but the Yankees swept four straight.

The annual All-Star Game was inaugurated the following year. Gabby was named catcher for the National League in that historic first game, and was the catcher for the first five years of the All-Star Game's existence. The 1934 contest was one of the most memorable games in Gabby's career.

He was the starting catcher, the Giants' Carl Hubbell the starting pitcher. The American League was the strong favorite, with a tremendous array of sluggers. There was Ruth, Gehrig, Gehringer, Foxx, Simmons, Dickey, Joe Cronin, Heinie Manush and Mickey Cochrane.

Sure enough, Gehringer opened the game with a single, and went to second when the ball was played badly. Manush walked. Up came Babe Ruth, and it appeared as though the tough American Leaguers were going to make short work of Hubbell.

Gabby went out to the mound to talk to Hubbell, joined there by the National League infield. Hubbell listened as Gabby talked quietly about pitching to Ruth. The huddle broke up and Hubbell went to work. His first pitch was a ball. Then he threw three straight strikes past the great Bambino. Up came Lou Gehrig. Gabby chirped encouragement from behind the plate. Hubbell struck Gehrig out swinging. Then he struck out Foxx.

The second inning, Hubbell struck out Simmons; then he struck out Cronin before Dickey ended the streak with a single. Lefty Gomez then fanned. Six strikeouts out of seven men, and five straight against the most powerful hitters in the American League. Catching those two All-Star innings was an experience Gabby never forgot. For years afterward he would replay those innings, pitch by pitch, for anyone who would listen.

Gabby had a good year at bat, an amazing year defensively in 1934. He hit .299, and committed only three errors all season, leading the league's catchers with a .996

fielding average. He was also tops in put-outs and assists for the season.

He came up with another tremendous season in 1935, the year Mickey Cochrane was driving the Detroit Tigers to their second straight pennant in the American League. Hartnett was doing his best to get the Cubs into the World Series against Cochrane's team, but by September Chicago was mired in third place, behind the Giants and Cardinals.

Then the Cubs began a 21-game winning streak that carried them right through the final game of the season, with Gabby pounding the ball at a near .400 clip in those three weeks. When it was all over, the Cubs had the pennant, and Gabby the National League's Most Valuable Player award. He hit .344 with 13 homers and 91 runs batted in, and again led the league's catchers in fielding.

Between the season's end and the awarding of the MVP, however, came the World Series. The Tigers, behind Cochrane, took the classic in six games. His second World Series homer did little to comfort Gabby, who had accomplished so much in his career, but never played on a World Series winner.

By now Gabby was an established institution in the league. He was without doubt its best catcher. Along with Dickey and Cochrane in the American League, he was recognized as one of the best three in baseball. It was, in fact, the era of the catcher; never in baseball history had three catchers so dominated the game as did Hartnett, Dickey and Cochrane. Not until the 1940's, when Berra and Campanella starred, had even two catchers of such eminence starred at the same time.

At a time when most ballplayers, especially catchers, were preparing to call it a career and pack it in, Gabby was reaching new heights. He was thirty-four years old when he won the MVP in 1935, actually just a few months shy of thirty-five. But he followed that with a .307 season in 1936 and, amazingly, a career high of .354 in 1937.

That was the year he took over the managerial reins of the Cubs. Midway through the season skipper Charley Grimm was taken ill, and Gabby was appointed interim manager. The decision was a tremendously popular one with the players, who liked Gabby to a man, and respected his baseball knowledge.

He was not a tough taskmaster, in the tradition of a John McGraw or a Joe McCarthy. Gabby was too good-humored for that. His first meeting as a manager, matter of fact, was filled with laughter, although he tried to be serious. Still, the Cubs had so much respect for him, no player took advantage of his good nature. They in fact gave a little extra, trying to make a success of the team for his sake.

Gabby, in turn, respected their professionalism. He never scolded a player, publicly or privately. On the other hand, his shrewd eyes never missed a thing. In pre-game meetings he would quietly point out mistakes that had been made the day before, then add some amusing comment to take any possible sting out of his criticism.

With his pitchers he was especially considerate, but they always knew he was the boss, and if he believed they were getting careless during a game he cracked down on them, in his own way. Veteran Charley Root told a sportswriter about it one day.

"Gabby didn't say much, as usual," Root said. "But if you let up during the game, or began getting grumpy, maybe, about how the ump was calling 'em, he'd fire that ball back at you like a shot. That would wake you up in a hurry, and get you back to business. The thing about Gabby is, he's always alert, and he means for his pitcher to be the same. I bet he's broken up more steals and hit-and-run plays by calling for pitch-outs than any other catcher in baseball."

The statistics indicated that Root was right. Gabby did hold the major league records for most years leading the league's catchers in assists and double plays, records earned by cuttting down base runners. He also held the World Series records for most assists and double plays in a four-game Series, records he set in 1932.

That year of 1937 he also set league records for most years catching one hundred or more games (twelve years), most years leading in fielding average (seven years).

When the new season started, Grimm was back as manager, and Gabby was hired as player and coach. At thirty-seven, he felt he needed more rest to play his best, and allowed Ken O'Dea to alternate with him behind the plate. However, on July 20, with the team playing below par, Grimm was fired, and Gabby named to manage the team once again.

"I'm as happy as a kid with a new toy," Gabby said at a press conference. "I only hope I'm as lucky as a manager as I have been as a player. If I am, we should be all right."

Though Gabby seemed the logical successor to Grimm to most baseball observers, there were some who thought the job would go to second baseman Tony Lazzeri. The former Yankee star had come to the Cubs after the 1937 season. Many felt that he was brought over to be groomed for the manager's job when Grimm left.

During the press conference naming Gabby as manager, the photographers tried to get Lazzeri and Hartnett to pose together. Lazzeri was suspicious. "I know what you want," he said. "You're gonna write under the pictures about how Gabby and I are gonna get along together, or not get along together. But all I've got to say is Gabby should have been made manager long ago. All I hope is that he'll find some place for me to get into the game every day so I can show him where I stand.

128

He's my friend, and he's gonna be a great manager."

Dizzy Dean, the former St. Louis Cardinals' pitching great, acquired that year at Hartnett's suggestion, was equally pleased with the change. For Dean's money, there wasn't a better catcher in baseball. In the All-Star Game the year before, Gabby had been Diz's catcher, and Dean had proclaimed afterward, "If I had that guy to pitch to all the time, I'd never lose me a game."

For a time in 1938, when he joined the Cubs, it seemed like there was some basis for the statement, for Dean won six straight before dropping his first decision.

The Cubs were in fourth place when Gabby took over. By August he had them in second, but in midmonth they still trailed the Pirates by eight games. Gabby wouldn't let them quit. He needled them amiably, and inspired them with his own unfailing courage and optimism. Dean was of little use in the latter part of the season, but Bill Lee and Clay Bryant pitched brilliantly down the stretch, narrowing the lead bit by bit. With two weeks to go the Pirates led by three and a half games. Then, with a week left, two games. Finally the two teams met in a climactic three-game series on September 27. The Pirates led by one and a half games.

Dizzy Dean made one of his rare effective appearances, beating the Pirates in the opener with help from Bill Lee in the ninth. With their backs to the wall and their once proud lead cut to half a game, the Pirates knocked Bryant out of the box in the next game and took a 3–1 lead in the sixth. The Cubs tied the score in their half, but the Pirates scored two more in the top half of the eighth. Again the Cubs tied the contest with a two-run rally.

Root set the Pirates down easily in the ninth. Mace Brown, the Bucs' relief pitcher, got Cavaretta and Carl Reynolds, and up to the plate stepped Gabby. The afternoon was growing dark. The umpires had already conferred and decided to call the game after the ninth should the score be tied.

Brown threw Gabby a curve. He took it for a strike. Another curve, and Gabby fouled it off.

In the darkness Brown figured he didn't need the usual waste pitch. He tried to throw his fast ball past Hartnett. Gabby was waiting for it. He swung. There was a sharp crack, and everybody in the ball park knew the ball was gone. It flew deep into the left-field seats for the game-winning homer.

It was, in effect, the pennant-winning homer. The blow broke the back of the Pirates, giving the Cubs a half-game lead. Two days later Chicago clinched the flag, beating the Cardinals, 10–3, while the Pirates were losing to the Reds. In their thrilling drive to the pennant, the Cubs had won twenty-one of their last twenty-five games.

Gabby was in the dugout for the pennant clincher, nursing two fingers split by foul tips. The index finger of his right hand was particularly blue and swollen. There was doubt that he would be ready for the World Series against the Yankees, but he was determined to play. "I'll get into that Series if they have to fit me with crutches," he said.

Again, however, the World Series proved to be a dismal disappointment for him. Few National League teams had much success against the Yankees in those years, and Hartnett's miracle Cubs were no different. The Yankees swept them four straight.

Gabby was a true "Iron Man" of baseball, very much in the tradition of Lou Gehrig. After the debacle of the 1938 season he remained with Chicago as playing manager for two more seasons, as the Cubs sank to fourth place, then fifth. In November of 1940, a month before his fortieth birthday, the Cubs released him.

At that age he was expected to seek employment

somewhere in baseball as a coach, if he couldn't land a job as a manager. Not Gabby. "I want to play," he said. "I'm not washed up yet. No reason I can't catch half a season for a couple more years yet."

The New York Giants believed him. They signed him on as a player-coach for the 1941 season. He got into sixty-four games for the Giants and hit .300, including five homers. He committed just one error in those sixty-four games, for a .994 fielding average.

That closed out Hartnett's major league career, after 1,990 games, a .297 lifetime average, and 236 home runs.

For five more years Gabby kicked around the minor leagues as a player-manager, piloting Indianapolis of the American Association, then the Jersey City Giants and finally Buffalo of the International League. He was forty-one years old when he skippered Indianapolis, but he got the old legs to carry him through seventy-two games behind the plate. Somehow he even managed to run out two triples that year. He was almost forty-four and managing at Jersey City before he put the bat and the catching tools away forever.

In 1955, Gabby was elected to the Hall of Fame.

Joe Torre

6

"BOY, are you fat!"

Many an overweight teen-age boy has heard these taunting words. Some feel shame, but get used to it; others are goaded into losing weight. In either case the obesity has usually created problems of personal appearance and health. But for sixteen-year-old Joe Torre, his stomach was literally getting in the way of a professional baseball career.

He stood there now, in the locker room of the Milwaukee Braves, stung by the remark just hurled at him by pitcher Warren Spahn. A moment ago he had entered the room with his older brother Frank, the Braves' first baseman, proud as Frank had introduced him as "my little big brother."

Then Spahn had plunged the harpoon into his flesh. He stood there, embarrassed, managing a feeble laugh. His brother said, "See, I told you you were a fat slob. Now maybe you'll believe me."

Joe seethed inwardly. His brother was always calling

him "a fat slob," at home in Brooklyn with the family, or in front of friends, and now in front of all these ballplayers of the Milwaukee Braves. He had to admit it was true enough; he weighed 240 pounds and was ringed with fat. Moreover, he realized, during those moments he stopped to think about it, that his brother's insults were meant to help him, meant to shame him into losing weight.

At that very moment, standing there in the visiting team's clubhouse at Ebbets Field, he thought it quite possible that Frank had put Spahn up to his opening remark.

The trouble was, Joe didn't know what to do about his weight. He loved to eat, especially the huge plates of pasta his mother prepared at the family's home in Brooklyn. He kept referring to his weight as "baby fat," hoping it would somehow disappear as he grew older. Instead it seemed to solidify. At first he almost welcomed the weight. He thought it had its effect on his hitting when he began playing serious amateur baseball on the Brooklyn sandlots. He showed tremendous power with the bat, even as a thirteen-year-old playing with the Cadets in Marine Park, across the street from his house. He thought of himself then as "husky," rather than fat, and thus able to hit the ball harder and farther than the other youngsters his age.

He played first base, emulating Frank, already an established professional, or third, and sometimes pitched. His powerful hitting very quickly became the talk of the organized sandlot leagues in Brooklyn, that same region which spawned a number of great baseball players, including a young pitcher then breaking in with the Dodgers, Sandy Koufax. Frank had played against him at the Parade Grounds, and Joe had watched many a duel between his big brother and the young, wild fireballer.

Because Frank was with the Braves, and their father

136

was now a major league scout, Honey Russell of the Braves went around to Brooklyn to see what the younger Torre brother looked like. He reported back to Milwaukee: "Too fat and too slow. He has absolutely no future."

Joe was fourteen when Russell looked at him. From that point on, Frank hammered away at him to lose weight, in vain. Joe continued to put away heaping portions of spaghetti, bang the ball over the sandlot fences and lose the interest of the major league scouts.

Even starring at first base for St. Francis Prep didn't win him any professional offers. He began to wonder why, still refusing to accept that his weight was that important. Then Frank brought him to Ebbets Field, that summer of 1960, to meet his teammates, and Spahn promptly stuck the harpoon into his flabby belly.

"Boy, are you fat!"

Joe swallowed the insult, as he had swallowed so many from his brother during the preceding years. Fred Haney, the Braves' manager, let him put on a uniform and work out with the team. He ran in the outfield, shagging flies, then took a turn in the batting cage. Pitching batting practice that day was Bob Buhl, one of the club's leading hurlers. Joe hit a few on the ground, then sent one of Buhl's pitchers rattling off the left-field wall.

"Nice going, fat boy," said Buhl.

Joe's day was ruined. He heard "fat boy" wherever he went. He was so embarrassed he wouldn't shower with the rest of the team, but waited until they took the field at game time.

At home that night, over dinner, Frank sailed into him again. Their parents and older brother Rocco, a policeman, listened as Frank related how Spahn, Buhl and the others had commented on Joe's weight. "And look at that pile of spaghetti and meatballs. And all that bread," Frank said.

"You wanna become a ballplayer, kid," he said to Joe, "you better become a catcher. You're too fat for anything else."

"Catcher!" snorted Joe. "That's no fun."

Thus Joe went his portly way, headed for nothing but oblivion, a budding baseball career being crushed under a burden of pasta and Italian bread.

When he was graduated from St. Francis Prep he was offered a baseball scholarship to St. John's University, but he thought surely he would receive an offer from some professional team that summer, and so declined the invitation. Instead he took a job as a page boy on the floor of the New York Stock Exchange, running messages.

No offers came. The scouts had given up on him. They all reported that he could hit, but would never make it to the major leagues because of his gross overweight.

Meanwhile, Joe continued to play with the Cadets, now in the amateur Federation League in Brooklyn. In the spring of 1959, just before his nineteenth birthday, the Torre family held a council of war. Something drastic had to be done, or Joe was finished as a baseball player before he'd even begun.

Frank again brought up the subject of catching. "Look, Joe," he said. "You're fat, and I'm not just giving you the needle now. But you're too slow to be a first baseman, or anything else but a catcher. You won't have to run fast. Just hit a little, and they'll pay you."

Their mother, Margaret, an avid baseball fan, agreed. "They could use a good catcher, too," she argued. "There's hardly more than two or three really good ones around."

This was true enough. With the exception of the Yankees' Yogi Berra and Elston Howard and the Braves' Del Crandall, the rest of the major league catching was little better than adequate. It seemed the logical position to go for.

Finally, Joe agreed to try. He went to Jim McElroy, manager of the Cadets, and told him he was through with first base, he wanted to catch. McElroy allowed him to alternate with the team's regular catcher.

Joe proved to be what is called a "natural." He fit into the position as though it had been designed for him, and he found to his pleasant surprise that he liked it behind the plate. Furthermore, the strenuous exercise he got there, under the hot New York sun, began to melt the pounds off him. By watching his diet as well, Joe reduced to 220. He was still substantially overweight, bulging particularly around the middle, but he was moving in the right direction.

Late that summer, under the persuasion of Frank, Honey Russell agreed to take another look at the younger Torre brother. What he saw amazed him; with just about fifty games' experience behind the plate the youngster showed the poise of a veteran. The Braves' scout realized at once that news of Joe's reformation would get around to other scouts, who visited the Brooklyn sandlots on a fairly regular basis. He decided on the spot to sign Joe to a Milwaukee contract.

Russell had little problem getting the contract signed. He was the scout who had signed Frank, and was trusted by the family. Joe was eager enough to quit his Wall Street job. For a bonus of about $20,000 he became the property of the Milwaukee Braves.

Joe reported to the rookie instructional camp in Florida that winter. For the first time he was seen by members of the Braves' executive staff. John McHale, the general manager, took one look at the portly young man and fired a cable to scout Honey Russell:

WHY DID YOU SIGN HIM. STOP. HE LOOKS LIKE A BOY BARTENDER.

139

Russell wired back: HE'LL BE A BETTER PLAYER THAN FRANK.

Braves farm director John Mullen was also horrified at the sight of Joe's flabby frame. "Man, are you fat!" he exclaimed. By now Joe was inured against such exclamations, however. Besides, he now had a contract in his possession, and the confidence that he would get into better shape and become a major leaguer.

Mullen worked him hard, trimming off the pounds, turning some of the fat into hard muscle. When Joe wasn't catching a game he was catching batting practice or shagging flies in a sweat suit. The strict regimen worked; he hit .340 in the instructional league games that winter. His work behind the plate improved tremendously. He was fit and hard, though still carrying a bit too much weight.

From the rookie camp he went directly to the Braves' regular spring training camp in Florida, a stipulation he had made when signing his bonus contract. When he walked into the dressing room, this time without the necessity of an introduction from his brother, he was at once greeted by Spahn, who said, "Hey, this can't be the same fat kid!"

Joe showed the Braves that indeed he was not. While hardly qualifying as a gazelle around the base paths, he nevertheless showed speed and grace behind the plate. He could throw quickly and accurately, he could catch, and he could hit better than ever.

After spring training he was sent to Eau Claire, in the Northern League, a Class C team. Bill Steinke, a crusty former major league catcher, began a basic catching course for the rookie. Shortly after the season opened, Steinke reported to the Braves on the youngster's possibilities.

"He can hit, and he's tough," said Steinke. "He won't quit on himself or you. He has tremendous desire and confidence. He'll be all right. He's having trouble catching the high inside pitch, but he'll catch on."

According to the Eau Claire manager, the high inside pitch was often a problem to inexperienced catchers, who have a tendency to blink. He worked with Joe to combat this fault. For example, the young catcher might be sitting in front of his locker, talking to someone, and Steinke would walk by and suddenly shove his hand in front of his face. The idea was to get him not to blink.

His first season of professional ball was a sensation. With the tough Steinke urging him ever onward, Joe caught 117 games, hit 16 homers and batted in 74 runs. On the final day of the season, tied with Max Alvis for the batting championship, he got six hits in a doubleheader to win with .344. He was named the league's Rookie of the Year.

With a few games remaining in the major leagues, the Braves brought him up and let him play the final innings of two games. His first time up in a major league uniform he singled off Harvey Haddix. The next time Bob Friend struck him out.

"Not bad, a .500 average for my first big league record," he said with a laugh.

As far as Steinke was concerned, Joe Torre was ready to settle down in the major leagues right then. The Braves did not quite agree. Besides, they had Crandall, one of the best catchers in baseball, with Charley Lau and Hawk Taylor on the bench behind him. There seemed to be no reason to rush Joe up to the majors, to sit in the dugout, when he could be gaining further experience by playing every day.

They promoted him to Louisville, in the American Association.

The season was barely a week old when Crandall developed a severe arm injury. Still the Braves were reluctant to bring up Torre. He was hitting well over .300

141

at Louisville, getting off to a torrid start. They didn't want to interrupt his progress. Lau took over behind the plate for the Braves, who thought Crandall would be sidelined for only a week. But a month later he was still out, and the Braves had no idea when he would return.

Under these circumstances, manager Charley Dressen felt obliged to call up Torre, who was hitting .342 for Louisville. Joe was in Omaha, that night of May 20, 1961, fast asleep, when the phone rang in his hotel room. It was Ben Geraghty, the Louisville manager.

"You're joining the Braves in Cincinnati right away," he said. "Get dressed and meet me in the lobby. I'll give you the details."

It was then about one o'clock in the morning, Geraghty told him he was to catch a plane to Chicago at 3:30, and there a connecting flight to Cincinnati at 7:25. Joe rushed back upstairs, awakened his roommate, pitcher Hank Fischer, shook his hand, packed his bags, and fled to the airport.

He arrived in time, only to find that his flight had been postponed to 4:50. When he finally landed in Chicago, his Cincinnati-bound plane was already in the air. He waited in the coffee shop, half-asleep, until the next flight, at 10:00. Shortly before noon he arrived in Cincinnati, checked in at the Braves' hotel, deposited his luggage and took a cab to Crosley Field. The game was due to start in half an hour.

"How do you feel?" asked Dressen.

"Fine," Joe said, "except that I haven't had any sleep." He explained the missed connections.

Dressen nodded. "Take the afternoon off, kid. Get some sleep. You can make it up tomorrow. We got a doubleheader. You can catch both games."

In a large sense it all seemed unreal to Joe. It was as though a daydream he had concocted and replayed many times in his mind had suddenly come to life, exactly the way he had always dreamed it. Four years earlier Warren Spahn, the great Warren Spahn, had called him, "fat boy." Now he was sitting with that same Warren Spahn in the clubhouse of the Milwaukee Braves, and one of the best pitchers in baseball history was saying to him, "You call your own game. If I don't agree I'll shake you off."

It was almost too much for him to accept, to comprehend. He actually felt himself shaking a bit. He had, after all, little more than a year of professional experience. He hadn't even been a catcher until two years ago. Now suddenly he was calling the signals for Warren Spahn, no less.

Inborn professional that he was, however, Torre got over his case of nerves soon after the action began. In the second inning Wally Post hit a high pop-up, one of the trickiest plays for a young catcher to make. Torre threw off his mask, got a good look at the ball, and caught it easily. From then on he knew he would be all right.

Actually, he was more than just all right that day. His debut as a regular big league catcher rivaled Roy Campanella's in its impact. He hit a single, a double and a homer in the doubleheader and threw out Vada Pinson, Frank Robinson and Eddie Kasko trying to steal.

He climaxed the performance with a defensive gem in the ninth inning of the second game. With two out and the Reds trailing by a run, Pinson tried to score the tying run on a base hit. As he came barreling home, the throw came in to Torre off the target, up the third base line. He grabbed the ball, lunged at Vinson, who sent him flying with his fullback charge. But Joe made the tag, and despite the fact that he was knocked down, held on to the ball for the final out.

"That," said Braves coach Andy Pafko, "is the action of a guy who's been here ten years."

As for Spahn, he shook Joe off just three times in the opening game. "He's an exceptional kid," the masterful left-hander said. "You forget how young he is."

Joe's one regret was that brother Frank was not there to see it and be part of it. Unfortunately for the elder Torre, scout Honey Russell's assessment had been accurate. By the time Joe broke in with Milwaukee, Frank was already down in Vancouver. Soon afterward he left baseball entirely, and joined Joe in a sporting goods business.

Though the Braves weren't going anywhere in 1961, eventually finishing fourth, their rookie catcher was on his way to a remarkable career. After making his sensational debut with Spahn, Torre experienced another memorable thrill with the great left-hander, later that season. With 299 victories, Spahn took the mound the night of August 11, looking for win number 300. Before the game, he and Torre talked things over.

"It's just another game," Spahn said, feeling the nervousness in the young catcher. "We've played the Cubs before."

Suddenly Torre realized that Spahn was as nervous as he was. It was, after all, more than just another game. It was an important milestone in an already historic career.

In the fifth inning of a scoreless tie, Torre doubled to left, advanced to third on an infield out, and scored on a fly ball by Spahn. The Cubs tied it in the sixth. A homer by Gino Cimoli in the eighth gave the edge back to the Braves, 2–1.

With two out in the ninth, the Cubs had Ernie Banks on first and Jim McAnany at the plate. Torre signaled for a screwball. Spahn shook him off, the first time he had done so all day. Torre came back with the sign for a fast ball. Spahn nodded, stretched, threw the fast ball. McAnany swung and lifted an easy fly ball to right.

When the ball was gathered in, Spahn jumped in the air and came down off the mound to give Joe a bear hug.

The veteran and the rookie. Reporters in the press box recalled that Joe Torre hadn't even been born when Warren Spahn won his first professional baseball game in 1940.

Crandall's injury kept him out of action for the remainder of the season, giving Joe a golden opportunity. He proved to the Braves that he was ready to take over as first-string catcher anytime they wanted him to. Catching 113 games in 1961, Joe batted .278, hit 10 home runs, and finished runner-up to the Cubs' Billy Williams for Rookie of the Year.

Crandall himself admitted Torre's talents were remarkable. "Joe is the finest young catcher I've seen come up to the big leagues since I've been here," he said.

Crandall made a complete recovery over the winter, and was ready to resume his catching job when the 1962 season began. As far as manager Birdie Tebbetts was concerned, there was no question of a rivalry for the position. Crandall was a veteran and one of the best, Torre a kid with plenty of time to learn. Joe was relegated to the bench, with the assurance that he and Crandall would split catching assignments through the season.

This wasn't enough for Joe, who wanted to play every day, who felt he wasn't at his best unless he played every day. Tebbetts, sensing the frustration, tried to get to him by telling a reporter one day, "Torre is going through the same procedure I did. I learned how to be a catcher by working under Mickey Cochrane. He's watching Crandall. Someday he'll be one of the greats at bat and behind the plate."

Joe played in eighty games in 1962, batting .282. He never uttered a public word of complaint. However, when the season was over, and it was announced that

Bobby Bragan would manage the club in 1963, Torre spoke out.

"In my heart I always felt I could have done better last year if Birdie had shown more confidence in me. I never knew from day to day whether I was going to play. I know Del Crandall is a great catcher," he said, "but I'm going to win the job."

Over the winter he served in the Air National Guard, and reported to spring training in better shape than ever, slimmer and hard. He won the catcher's job from Crandall, who was put at first base by Bragan. Then, after a while, Bragan decided to experiment with a switch.

"Get the first baseman's glove," he told Torre one day, "and let's see how that works."

Joe didn't mind. He knew that the catcher's job was essentially his, and playing first base was a break in the routine. Besides, it gave him a kind of specal satisfaction.

"I'm getting a kick out of it," he told a sportswriter one day, "and my old manager on the Cadets, Jim McElroy, must be getting a chuckle out of it as well. When I played the sandlot leagues the scouts said I could never play first base in the major leagues."

Manager Bragan, another former major league catcher, was as impressed with Torre at first as he was with him behind the plate. "He's got good hands," he said, "and goes to his right very well. I've never seen a young right-handed first baseman make that tough first-to-second-to-first double play as well."

Nevertheless, after a brief period at first, and even a few games in the outfield, Bragan put Torre back where he really belonged—behind the plate. It was as catcher he was named to the National League All-Star team in 1963, though he didn't get into the game.

Toward the latter part of the season, it became apparent that Del Crandall was superfluous with Joe Torre

146

around. It made no sense to keep two first-rate catchers on the roster. It was apparent, too, that it was Crandall who would go; the Braves recognized in Torre the makings of a superstar. He was not only a rugged receiver, but a tremendous hitter, a line-drive hitter who could hit for a good average as well as with power.

"He waits until the ball gets on top of him," Braves coach George Myatt said one day. "There aren't many hitters around who can do that."

He hit a home run off Sandy Koufax in Los Angeles one day that Koufax talked about for weeks afterward. He hit it to straightaway center field, where the wall is 410 feet from home plate.

"When the ball went out there on a line I wasn't worried," Koufax said afterward. "I figured it's got a long way to go. But it kept going and going and going, right over the wall, and for all I know it's still going."

Torre was proving that he was just as tough behind the plate. He showed in his first season that he had an accurate, consistent arm. Base runners took no liberties. Now in his third season he was demonstrating the durability needed to make a great catcher. The bruises and scars of the catching trade were beginning to accumulate, but he would shake them off and come right back, tougher than ever.

One of the toughest tests for a young catcher is the "bang-bang" play, the moment he has to take a throw from right field just as the runner from third is charging into the plate. Torre held up well in his very first game, when he tagged out Vada Pinson on such a play in Cincinnati.

But Johnny Temple of the Houston Astros really put him to the test—three times in one season.

The first time Temple charged in head first, and was tagged out. The second time he leaped into Joe, drove his knees into his chest, and tore open his pants with his spikes. Temple won that round; Torre dropped the ball and was nearly knocked unconscious. But he rose, shakily, asked for time while he changed his pants, and continued in the game.

On the third encounter Temple charged in again and kneed Torre in the groin. This time Joe sent Temple sprawling and tagged him out.

Twice that season, too, he had his finger split by a foul tip, but refused to quit. He did miss one game, however, or at least part of one game. In a play at the plate Julian Javier of the Cardinals slid in and ripped open his knee with flashing spikes. Torre tagged him out, then allowed himself to be taken to the hospital to have the wound stitched. Afterward he caught a cab back to the ball park to watch the end of the game.

"What's so unusual about that?" he replied to a sportswriter's question about his swift return. "If you're a baseball player and you can walk, you belong in the ball park."

Torre finished the 1963 season with a .293 average, 14 home runs and 71 runs batted in. Extra proof of his power was the fact that he hit four triples. For a man of his size and speed, the ball had to kick around the farthest reaches of the ball park to enable him to chug around to third.

"Now I want to hit three hundred," he said. "There aren't many catchers around who hit three hundred."

As expected, the Braves traded Crandall. He went to San Francisco, as part of a deal that brought catcher Ed Bailey over to back up Torre.

"I may play Joe at first base against right-hand pitching," Bragan announced. "That way I can get his and Bailey's bats in the game."

Playing in 154 games, more games than anyone in the league that season, he also led the league catchers in fielding percentage, with .994. He caught part of the All-

Star Game and, as Bragan had figured, played first base when Bailey was behind the plate.

He completely dominated the catching in both leagues. In the American League the Yankees' Elston Howard, MVP the year before, came back with a .313 average. Torre hit .321, the first National League catcher to hit more than .300 since Roy Campanella did it in 1955. In addition he hit 20 homers, 5 triples and batted in 109 runs.

In the spring of 1965, under the broiling sun of West Palm Beach, as Torre took intensive batting practice, a small knot of interested parties watched him from the shade of the dugout. Bill Steinke, his manager at Eau Claire, was one of the men.

"He's a classic old plate blocker, that boy," Steinke said. "He's in the tradition of Cochrane, and Hartnett, and Dickey. He's clean, but if he has to tag you, you know you've been tagged."

"He's tough all right," said Joe Garagiola, who grew up with Yogi Berra and later caught with the Cardinals. A sports broadcaster since retiring from baseball, he had ample opportunity to watch everything going on in the major leagues. "If I had to pick one man to start a franchise," Garagiola went on, "it would be Torre. You could build a whole club around him. He's the best catcher in the world, and then you could play him at first base and win, too."

"How would you rate him as a handler of pitchers?" somebody asked.

"Tops," said Steinke.

Garagiola laughed. "Listen," he said, "all this guy has to do is not shave, and then you get some kid in there, squinting in for the sign, and baby, that's no Rembrandt he's seeing. He's got to be more scared of Torre than the batter."

Even veteran Braves pitchers could attest to Torre's ferocity when he believed it was needed to keep a hurler going. There was the day Tony Cloninger began to tire in the ninth inning, holding on to a slim lead against the Cardinals. Torre noticed that he was not coming down with a full follow-through. He went out to the mound briskly.

"Bend your back!" he said sharply.

"What do you think I'm doing?" retorted Cloninger.

"I said bend your back!" snarled Torre.

Cloninger was furious, so furious he struck out the side to end the game.

There was the time, too, when Torre knew how to blend just the right amounts of callousness with humor. Wade Blasingame had a no-hitter going against the Mets when a single in the eighth inning ruined it. Out to the mound came Torre. He knew Blasingame tended to get down on himself, and when he did, he was belted out of the park. This was just such a moment.

Blasingame stood on the mound, dejected, looking for sympathy from his catcher and roommate. Torre came up to him and said, "Forget it. You're too young to have a no-hitter anyway. So let's get this over with and go home."

Blasingame sailed through the rest of the Mets to nail down the victory.

Joe began the 1965 season in a tremendous burst of power, slamming extra-base hits and homers at every ball park. One day in early May, he was taking batting practice at Shea Stadium, sending pitch after pitch rattling off the fences or into the seats. High upstairs, from their vantage point in the Diamond Club, general managers John McHale of the Braves and George Weiss of the Mets watched Torre hit.

"How much do you want for him?" Weiss asked.

"He's not for sale. Not at any price," said McHale.

"Any price?" said Weiss. "How about half a million dollars."

"Not at any price," repeated McHale.

The Mets could have used Torre on many counts. They always had catching troubles, among their many problems. Moreover, as a Brooklyn boy, he would be an extra added attraction. And finally, he seemed to make it a point to personally ruin the Mets every time he played Shea Stadium.

On Mother's Day, that very month, he had one of the finest days of his career. The day before, his sister, a nun, had given him a St. Joseph's medal. On Mother's Day itself his mother came out to see him play. Before going on the field for the first game of the doubleheader, he pinned the St. Joseph's medal to the inside of his left sleeve. He got a single and a homer in the first game.

In the second game, he popped up on his first time at bat. Suddenly he realized that between games he had changed shirts. He sent the batboy into the clubhouse for the medal and pinned it to his sleeve again.

He got four straight hits after that, including two more home runs. He's worn the St. Joseph's medal pinned to his sleeve ever since.

"I need all the help I can get," he said after the doubleheader.

Gene Oliver, the team's second-string catcher, Bailey having been released that month, shook his head at Joe's remark. "Actually, that guy doesn't need any help. He's the best right-handed hitter in baseball. When he's not getting hits he's hitting line-drive outs. He's the greatest, not only as a player, but as a man. He gets along with everybody."

Manager Bobby Bragan agreed. "He's the best in the business. I don't care what yardstick you want to use.

He's the best at hitting, the best at catching, the best at throwing."

Again Torre was named the National League catcher for the All-Star Game, played that year at Metropolitan Stadium, home of the Minnesota Twins.

Willie Mays opened the ball game by hitting a homer off Milt Pappas of the Orioles. Then, with two out and Willie Stargell on first, Torre came up and got his first All-Star Game hit, a home run into the left-field seats. The National League won the game, 6–5.

Catching 100 games and playing 48 at first base, Torre hit .291 in 1965, with 80 runs batted in and 27 homers. As usual, however, the Braves weren't going anywhere that year—except to Atlanta. After thirteen years as a Milwaukee franchise, following their long history in Boston, the Braves were on the move again. In 1966 they became the Atlanta Braves.

Torre found the change very much to his liking. At once he began spraying home runs into the seats of the new park. Two weeks after the season opened, he beat the Mets, 5–4, batting in three runs with two homers. Five times that season he hit two homers in a game, and he hit a grand slammer in the first inning of Tracey Stallard that beat the Cardinals in mid-July.

The Braves were actually considered strong pennant contenders in their new surroundings, but couldn't get going, despite boasting the strongest homer-hitting line-up in the league. They spent most of the season in seventh or eighth place. Finally, in August, Bragan was fired as manager, and coach Billy Hitchcock put in charge.

The Braves came to life suddenly. Slugger Ed Mathews, who didn't get along with Bragan, was restored to full-time duty at third base. Later that month Torre surpassed his previous season's home run total by blasting his twenty-eighth of the season. Then he hit two against the Mets, to beat them, 6–3, and an eighth inning homer with two on to beat the Reds, 4–1.

Led by the slugging of Torre and Hank Aaron, the Braves put together a hot streak of victories, winning 8 straight and 19 out of 21, finishing the season in fifth place. Torre, with a .315 average, tied Willie Stargell for sixth spot in the league's batting race. He also hit a lifetime high of 36 homers, and batted in 101 runs. His slugging average of .560 was fourth best in the league, four points better than Willie Mays'.

As the best catcher in baseball, Torre felt that surely he should at least be the highest paid in the league. After a brief disagreement with the management, he signed for $65,000, best in the league, and second best on the Braves, where Hank Aaron ruled with a $100,000 contract.

He began the 1967 season as though he meant to break all previous records. On April 15 he personally demolished Juan Marichal of the Giants. With the Braves trailing, 1–0, he tied the score with a double, then scored the lead run on a single by Clete Boyer. The Giants tied the score in the sixth. In the eighth, with one out and Mack Jones on first, he walloped one of Marichal's fast balls over the left-field fence, his second homer of the young season. The Braves held on to win, 4–3.

A month later, against the Mets, he smashed six hits for twelve total bases in the course of a doubleheader. He hit a homer and two doubles in the first game, a double and two singles in the second game.

A series of minor injuries descended upon him like the plague, however, hampering his usually whiplike swing. He finished the season at .277, with twenty homers, figures that would have pleased most catchers in both leagues. To Joe Torre, they were bad marks to overcome in the future.

Unhappily, the next season began on similarly sour notes. First a pulled hamstring muscle sidelined him. Then, on April 18 of the 1968 season, he was beaned, and had to be put on the disabled list.

While there was serious cause for worry in the Braves' camp, as well as the Torre household, there was ample reason for optimism, too. Twenty-eight years old, the best catcher in baseball, indeed, marked by many as one of the true all-time greats, Joe Torre was considered a good bet to come back strong, with many years ahead of him behind the plate.

Testimonials to ballplayers from a manager or from teammates are to be expected. The true measure of a testimonial is appreciated when it is given by an enemy player. Maury Wills, certainly the greatest base runner of modern times, gives his to Torre. The two have been battling for years, with the score about even. Wills has little regard for catchers as a whole, regarding them as arch rivals who will do anything to cut him down.

His rivalry with Torre has been something else. "He has the quickest, most accurate, most consistent arm in the league," Wills said of him. "And he's clean. I've put my spikes through his shinguards, and once gashed his knee so badly he needed six stitches after the game. But at the time all he said was, 'I'm okay, let's go.' He could really have let me have it, but he just shook it off.

"Joe Torre is the only catcher in the league I even speak to."

Elston Howard

7

TO the author, to a great many baseball observers, sportswriters and veteran players, Bill Dickey, Yogi Berra, Roy Campanella, Mickey Cochrane and Gabby Hartnett stand as the five all-time great catchers of baseball. Similarly, Joe Torre is tops among active catchers, with an excellent chance of becoming Hall of Fame material. Certainly there have been many other fine catchers in baseball worthy of special mention, catchers with their personal champions who would have placed them among the top five.

There were Johnny Kling, Roger Bresnahan, Al Lopez, Ernie Lombardi, Ray Schalk, Wally Schang and Muddy Ruel among the old-timers, and Elston Howard among current catchers.

For several years, before young Torre became a star for the Braves, Howard was the best catcher in baseball. His story is a special one, not only because he was one of the outstanding receivers in the game but because he was the first Negro to play for the Yankees, and the first to win the Most Valuable Player Award in the American League.

Howard was "Special: Handle With Care," from the moment the Yankees began to scout him. That was in 1950, when he was a catcher-outfielder with the Kansas City Monarchs, in Negro baseball. By that time the other New York teams, the Giants and the Dodgers, were well integrated. The Yankees had no colored players, or any on their way up through the farm system. Sharply criticized for what appeared to be a segregationist attitude, the Yankees' answer was that they would not hire a colored ballplayer just for the sake of having one, or to silence critics. They would have one when they found one suitable.

Yankee scouts believed they had found such a man in Elston Howard. He appeared to fit the Yankee image. Born and brought up in St. Louis, Howard had a good school record, his father was a high school teacher, and he had a spotless personal background. The Yankees were not looking for a flamboyant, volatile type like Jackie Robinson. They wanted a player who would fit comfortably into the conservative Yankee flannels.

In June of 1950, while on the road with the Monarchs, Howard was signed by Johnny Neun, a Yankee scout, and sent to Muskegon, Michigan, where he spent the rest of the season playing the outfield. He was promoted to Binghamton after a .283 season in Muskegon, but the Korean War interrupted his career. He spent two years in Japan before returning to baseball. When he did, he found a catcher's mitt waiting for him.

"Try it on for size," scout Bill Skiff said to him in spring training. "We're gonna make a catcher out of you."

To help Howard, Bill Dickey came over from Sarasota, where the Yankees trained, to Lake Wales, where their farms teams trained. Dickey had made a catcher out of Yogi Berra, he would do the same for Howard. Dickey spent several weeks teaching him the rudiments of catching, for though Howard had worked behind the plate for the Monarchs, he had never had any formal training in the position.

Yet when he was sent to play with the Kansas City Blues for the 1953 season, Howard was still an outfielder. Except for a two-week period when one catcher was injured and the other in a slump, manager Harry Craft didn't let him catch. Howard began to wonder why the Yankees had bothered training him with Dickey.

Howard wasn't the only one wondering. There were some who thought that the Yankees were shuffling Howard around the minor leagues, stalling about bringing him up, using his lack of catching experience as an excuse, when they could in fact use him as an outfielder, his natural position.

In Florida in 1954, manager Casey Stengel denied it all vehemently. "He's too slow to make good as an outfielder," Casey told everybody. "He's gotta make it as a catcher. And he can do it, too."

The natural question was, then why hadn't he been used as a catcher in Kansas City?

"He was supposed to break in as a catcher there," Casey replied, "but that other young feller, Al Robertson, came along so fast we couldn't get this feller in there behind the plate so we kept him in the outfield."

His training resumed that spring, after which he was scheduled to go to Toronto, in the International League. Just before the season began Dickey said to Stengel, "He'll be a good one, all right. He's got all the natural gifts. The rest he'll have to get from experience."

Howard proved in Toronto that year that he was ready for the major leagues, and ready to make it as a catcher as well. Behind the plate for most of the 1954 season, he hit .330 for the Maple Leafs, second best in the league, led the league in triples with 16 and batted in 109 runs. Easily he won the International League's Most Valuable Player award.

The Yankees could have used that bat in 1954. After five straight pennants, they lost to the Indians. Said pitcher Allie Reynolds after the season's finale: "If we'd had Howard we would've made it six straight!"

There was no holding Howard back any longer. He came up to the Yankees in 1955, understudied Yogi Berra for a while, then gradually took over the catching duties as Yogi began to fade. In 1961 he batted .348 and hit 21 homers, and appeared headed for an MVP award. That was the year Roger Maris won it, however, by hitting 61 home runs for a new major league record.

Two years later Howard got his MVP. There was nobody else really in contention. From the beginning of the season he was the one man in the Yankee lineup manager Ralph Houk could depend upon for regular service. During the opening weeks he was almost solely responsible for keeping the team close to the top of the league, breaking out in a home run streak that won ball games.

Injuries and hitting slumps had Houk playing the lineup like a vaudeville juggler. Howard was the only man hitting consistently, and on top of that he was handling the pitching staff with expert skill. To bolster the mound corps that spring Houk brought Al Downing up from Richmond. Howard took him in hand and made a winner out of him.

He in fact took over the entire team and made it a winner. Somebody had to take charge. Mickey Mantle and Roger Maris were in and out of the lineup. Berra was more coach than player. In terms of sheer experience he often found himself to be the senior man in the field.

The younger players looked to him for leadership, and he gave it to them.

The rest of the league thought the Yankees were dead without Maris and Mantle regularly in the lineup, but Howard was proving them wrong. Slowly the team moved upward in the standings, overtaking Baltimore, Cleveland and Minnesota. Only the White Sox were in front of them now, one game ahead, as they pulled into Chicago for a four-game series.

Whitey Ford pitched the first game, against Chicago's Juan Pizzaro. At the end of seven innings, the White Sox led, 2–1. With two out in the eighth, Tom Tresh beat out an infield hit. Howard then blasted a homer for a 3–2 lead. Ford held the margin, and the Yankees were tied for first place.

The next day Gary Peters restored the White Sox lead. But in a Sunday doubleheader Howard took it away again. He hit two home runs in the opener to help Jim Bouton beat Ray Herbert, 8–4; catching both games, his triple and single then helped Downing win, 6–2. The Yankees were in front by one game.

It was all Howard that year. Through the first three months of the 1963 season the Yankees' regular squad was in action only ten times; yet, amazingly, they were beginning to run away from the rest of the league.

"That Howard killed us," moaned Billy Hitchcock, the Orioles' manager, after losing three straight to the Yankees.

"To beat the Yankees," remarked Chicago manager Al Lopez, himself a former catching star, "you've got to outpitch them. And I gotta give that Howard credit; he really keeps those kids on their toes out there."

By the time slugging stars Maris and Mantle returned together to the lineup it was Labor Day; Howard had 28 homers and the Yankees were ten and a half games out in front. There was little left to do but play out the month and collect the pennant. When it was all over, Howard stood out as the club leader with a .287 average, 28 homers and 85 runs batted in. Mantle and Maris between them that season had only 38 homers and 88 runs batted in. Every player who had been with the Yankees in 1962 performed worse in 1963 with the exception of Howard.

The 1963 World Series was a memorable one for the Yankees only in the extent of the disaster. Fantastic Dodger pitching by Sandy Koufax and Don Drysdale beat them four straight times, the worst World Series humiliation in Yankee history. The team batting average was .171. Only Howard could hit the two great Dodger pitchers, batting .333, and accounting for 5 of the team's total of 22 hits.

Without Howard, the entire season for the Yankees would have ended in similar disaster.

On November 6, 1963, Elston Howard got his historic call. He was named MVP for the American League.

Howard had one more big season for the Yankees, hitting .313 in 1964, before he began to slip. At thirty-six, he found that while he could catch as well as ever, his hitting was suffering. After two more full seasons, the Yankees traded him to the Red Sox in August of 1967.

Boston manager Dick Williams wasn't waiting for Howard's bat. He had the big hitters, like Carl Yastrzemski and Tony Conigliaro. What he wanted was a team leader, a catcher who could guide the young pitchers, and work well with the veterans.

Precisely how much he valued Howard behind the plate he demonstrated during a game at Yankee Stadium on August 28. The Red Sox were leading, 2–0, Howard driving in one of the runs against his former mates, when pitcher Dave Morehead got into trouble. Williams took him out and replaced him with Sparky Lyle. But first he gave the young hurler a warning.

"Twice before you've gone in and shaken off Howard's signs. Well, you can do it again if you want to, but it will cost you fifty dollars."

Lyle didn't shake Howard off this time. He came on, struck out Steve Whitaker and got Charlie Smith on a ground out to end the threat. The Red Sox, on their way to the pennant, won the game, 3–0.

Afterward, in the clubhouse, manager Williams expanded on his admonition to Lyle. "With very few exceptions I've told my pitchers what Ellie puts down, they throw. And that's it."

After his long and distinguished career as a batsman, as well as fine fielding catcher, Howard didn't want to linger on as a .178 hitter, which was all he could manage in 1967. But Williams and the Red Sox management prevailed on him to come back in 1968.

"Without Ellie we wouldn't have won the pennant," Williams said. "We need him behind the plate, even if he hits zero."

Howard came back, and though Boston's fortunes dipped considerably, his own improved. Thirty-nine years old, he was in there catching regularly, and hitting as well as he had in many previous years. What the future held for him he didn't know, but surely there would always be need for a man like Elston Howard somewhere in baseball.

Duke Bresnahan

8

WHEN Roger Bresnahan died in the winter of 1944, a wonderful bit of baseball legend went with him. Roger, known around the baseball world as the Duke of Tralee, because that little town in Ireland was supposedly his birthplace, was the last survivor of one of the game's most famous triumvirates. In passing, he followed his old batterymate, Christy Mathewson, and his manager, the immortal John McGraw. Together these three had made the New York Giants of old one of the most colorful and powerful teams in baseball annals.

There were better catchers who followed Bresnahan into baseball in later years, though there are those who argue that he played in the era of the "dead ball" and would have been the best ever had he played in modern times. The point is moot. However, there is this to be said for certain. Never has there been a more versatile catcher, or one fleeter of foot. Bresnahan was like a fifth infielder.

He was in fact a pitcher, not a catcher, when he began playing baseball. A chunky lad of sixteen, actually born and brought up in Toledo (some imaginative later historian gave the Irish hero an Irish birthplace), he found he could earn money playing professional baseball with a team in Manistee, Michigan. That was in 1895. For the next few years he bounced around in what was then fairly disorganized professional baseball, playing for Lima, Ohio, for Washington in the old National League, for Toledo and Minneapolis and then with the Cubs, again in the National League.

Fast and rugged and a good hitter, Bresnahan played anywhere, but he preferred to pitch. It was essentially as a pitcher that he jumped to John McGraw's American League Orioles in 1901, when McGraw first put a club into that city. Rog also played the infield or the outfield when McGraw asked him to.

"Bresnahan is my troubleshooter," McGraw used to say. "Wherever I need a good man, he plays, and he plays like the devil."

One of the few positions Bresnahan skipped was catcher. Wilbert Robinson, later the famous "Uncle Willie" of zany Brooklyn Dodger fame, was McGraw's catcher.

During the 1901 season, Robinson broke his finger. The second-string catcher was out sick. The third-string catcher was so weak-armed he could barely reach the mound with his return throws. Bresnahan, hurling against this handicap one day, lost his patience and yelled at McGraw, who was playing third, "Why don't you get us a catcher?"

McGraw, the Little Napoleon, as he was called, walked over to the mound. "If you're so smart, Rog," he said with biting sarcasm, "why don't you catch yourself?"

Angrily Bresnahan threw away his glove and stomped

behind the plate, took away the catcher's mitt and stood there defiantly.

McGraw called his bluff. He called Iron Man McGinnity off the bench to pitch, and let Bresnahan stay behind the plate.

The Duke remained there for eighteen years.

Neither Bresnahan nor McGraw lasted long in Baltimore. In those early days of baseball the rules and contracts were less rigidly drawn, competition among teams and between leagues was wide open. Accordingly, when McGraw got into a series of arguments with the Orioles' owners, he jumped to the New York Giants of the National League right in the middle of the 1902 season. He took with him, among others, Bresnahan.

It was there that Rog teamed up with the great Christy Mathewson, and there, too, that he added something new to the catching game. He invented and wore the first shin guards ever donned by a catcher. At first he spent most of his playing days with the Giants patrolling the outfield, for Frank Bowerman was Mathewson's regular catcher. But after a while Matty asked for Bresnahan, and they became one of the classic duets in baseball.

That first full season in New York, 1903, McGraw took the cellar-dwelling Giants and engineered them into second place. Bresnahan played a major role in that spectacular rise. He hit .350, the best average of his life. What's more, that incredible speed of his, especially for a catcher, was revealed by his successful steal of 34 bases!

There was no World Series in 1904, when McGraw won his first pennant for the Giants, but the following season, operating under the new rules, the Giants and Athletics met for the first real World Championship.

And what a World Series that was! Again demonstrating that remarkable speed, Bresnahan was given the leadoff spot in the batting order, the only catcher ever to get that batting post. But the first classic turned out to be a pitchers' Series, every decision a shutout victory. More particularly, it was Mathewson's Series, for he won three of the four shutouts hurled against the Athletics. McGinnity threw the other one, as the Giants won in five games.

Bresnahan, besides catching the four shutouts, hit .313, second highest Giant mark of the Series.

While the Giants chased the Cubs in vain through the next three seasons, the St. Louis Cardinals, under the direction of John McCloskey, finished seventh once and last twice. In desperation, Stanley Robison, the St. Louis owner, asked the league to help him find a capable manager.

Rog expressed keen interest in the job. McGraw was his hero, and he was anxious to emulate the Little Napoleon. In a complicated three-way deal that also involved the Reds, McGraw let Bresnahan go to St. Louis as catcher-manager, getting in return the old spitballer, Bugs Raymond, outfielder Jack Murray and catcher George Schlei.

The appointment of Bresnahan created quite a stir in St. Louis. Big things were expected. But Rog couldn't carry a second-rate team alone. In his first two seasons he could only better their position by one place, but in 1911 he had the Cardinals in the thick of the pennant race for most of the season. The team eventually finished fifth, but the club owners were so pleased with Bresnahan's work they gave him a bonus and a new five-year contract. When he finished sixth the following year, however, he was fired, contract or no contract. In the squabble that followed, he wound up as player-manager for the Cubs.

After three years in Chicago, Rog longed to buy his own club and run it as he saw fit. He had saved a bit of his money, and invested it in the purchase of Toledo, in the Federal League. This was his birthplace, and this was where he wanted to spend his remaining days in baseball. He was thirty-seven years old when he took over, and still playing part time. He managed a .275 average while catching 40 games in 1917, before bowing out a year later.

He retained his interests in the club, however, until 1923, when he sold out. A free agent again, he was promptly hired by his old friend and former manager, McGraw, and he served as a coach under him for four seasons. His last baseball job was as coach in 1930 and 1931—for the Tigers. Then he retired to Toledo business interests.

When he died in December of 1944, he was still waiting for one of his life's ambitions to be realized; he wanted to be elected to the Hall of Fame. One year afterward the fabulous Duke of Tralee finally made it.

It is always difficult, in a sense impossible really, to compare ballplayers of widely different eras, for so many different factors enter into such comparisons: the ball changed, rules changed, bat construction changed, dimensions of the ball parks changed, the strike zone changed, even the gloves changed.

Certainly Roger Bresnahan was one of the finest catchers of his time, and one of the finest of all time. Some whose career spanned several baseball generations, men like McGraw and Branch Rickey, claim Bresnahan was the best of all time. Hans Wagner, perhaps the greatest shortstop who ever lived, went even further than McGraw or Rickey. Before he died in 1955, in a conversation with a sportswriter, he said of Bresnahan: "The first man I'd select on any all-time all-star team would be Bresnahan. He could do anything. He could catch, pitch, play the infield or the outfield. He could hit, throw and run. I'd say he was the most talented and versatile player in the history of the sport."

9

JOHNNY KLING of the Cubs has his adherents who think he belongs among the all-time greats. He, too, was one of the stars of the dead ball era. He was known as Mr. Brains of that old Chicago team, helping them to pennants in 1906, 1907, 1908 and 1910. Kling had an arm like a whip, in that department rating above Bresnahan. His career batting average was lower than Roger's, .271 to .279, but his handling of pitchers and overall field generalship were superb. The Cubs had a great pitching staff in those years—Mordecai Brown, Orvie Overall, Jack Pfeister and Ed Reulbach among the leaders—and all of them gave Kling much of the credit for their success.

"Schnoz" Lombardi

10

ON hitting alone Ernie "The Schnoz" Lombardi deserves mention in any listing of all-time great catchers, though he was an excellent receiver as well. Ernie was undoubtedly the slowest man in baseball, yet he retired with a lifetime batting average of .306. He was so slow he was forced to bat against what was virtually a seven-man outfield, for the infielders knew they could throw him out at first from several steps back on the grass. Could he have legged out a few hits, it's very likely he would have been a .400 hitter; he hit well into the .300's many times.

The classic tale of "Schnoz" Lombardi's tortoise pace is the one about the newspaper coverage he got the day he finally crossed up one of those infield-outfield defenses. Newspapers in Cincinnati, where he starred for the Reds, proclaimed the event in bold headlines on the sports pages: LOMBARDI BEATS OUT BUNT!

There you have them: Heroes Behind the Mask, all of them.

Records

LIFETIME RECORD: LAWRENCE PETER (YOGI) BERRA

Born May 12, 1925, St. Louis, Missouri

Batted left, threw right

Year Club	League	Pos.	G.	AB.	R.	H.	2B.	3B.	HR.	RBI.	B.A.
1943—Norfolk	Pied.	C	111	376	52	95	17	8	7	56	.253
1944-45—Kansas City	A.A.	(In Military Service)									
1946—Newark	Int.	C-OF	77	277	41	87	14	1	15	59	.314
1946—New York	Amer.	C	7	22	3	8	1	0	2	4	.364
1947—New York	Amer.	C-OF	83	293	41	82	15	3	11	54	.280
1948—New York	Amer.	C-OF	125	469	70	143	24	10	14	98	.305
1949—New York	Amer.	C	116	415	59	115	20	2	20	91	.277
1950—New York	Amer.	C	151	597	116	192	30	6	28	124	.322
1951—New York	Amer.	C	141	547	92	161	19	4	27	88	.294
1952—New York	Amer.	C	142	534	97	146	17	1	30	98	.273
1953—New York	Amer.	C	137	503	80	149	23	5	27	108	.296
1954—New York	Amer.	C-3B	151	584	88	179	28	6	22	125	.307
1955—New York	Amer.	C	147	541	84	147	20	3	27	108	.272
1956—New York	Amer.	C-OF	140	521	93	155	29	2	30	105	.298
1957—New York	Amer.	C-OF	134	482	74	121	14	2	24	82	.251
1958—New York	Amer.	C-OF-1B	122	433	60	115	17	3	22	90	.266
1959—New York	Amer.	C-OF	131	472	64	134	25	1	19	69	.284
1960—New York	Amer.	C-OF	120	359	46	99	14	1	15	62	.276
1961—New York	Amer.	OF-C	119	305	62	107	11	0	22	61	.271
1962—New York	Amer.	C-OF	86	232	25	52	8	0	10	35	.224
1963—New York	Amer.	C	64	147	20	43	6	0	8	28	.293
1964—New York†	Amer.	(Did not play—served as manager)									
Major League Totals			2116	7546	1174	2148	321	49	358	1430	.285

† Released by New York Yankees, October 16, 1964; signed as coach with New York Mets, November 17, 1964.

WORLD SERIES RECORD

Year Club	League	Pos.	G.	AB.	R.	H.	2B.	3B.	HR.	RBI.	B.A.
1947—New York	Amer.	C.-OF	6	19	2	3	0	0	1	2	.158
1949—New York	Amer.	C	4	16	2	1	0	0	0	1	.063
1950—New York	Amer.	C	4	15	2	3	0	0	1	2	.200
1951—New York	Amer.	C	6	23	4	6	1	0	0	0	.261
1952—New York	Amer.	C	7	28	2	6	1	0	2	3	.214
1953—New York	Amer.	C	6	21	3	9	1	0	1	4	.429
1955—New York	Amer.	C	7	24	5	10	1	0	1	2	.417
1956—New York	Amer.	C	7	25	5	9	2	0	3	10	.360
1957—New York	Amer.	C	7	25	5	8	1	0	1	2	.320
1958—New York	Amer.	C	7	27	3	6	3	0	0	2	.222
1960—New York	Amer.	C-OF-PH	7	22	6	7	0	0	1	8	.318
1961—New York	Amer.	OF	4	11	2	3	0	0	1	3	.273
1962—New York	Amer.	C	2	2	0	0	0	0	0	0	.000
1963—New York	Amer.	PH	1	1	0	0	0	0	0	0	.000
World Series Totals			75	259	41	71	10	0	12	39	.274

RECORD AS MANAGER

Year	Club	League	Pos.	W.	L.
1964—New York		American	First	99	63

WORLD SERIES RECORD

Year	Club	League	W.	L.
1964—New York		American	3	4

Manager, New York Yankees, 1964; Coach, New York Mets, 1965.
Voted Most Valuable Player, 1951, 1954, 1955.

179

LIFETIME RECORD: ROY CAMPANELLA

Born November 19, 1921, Philadelphia, Pa.

Batted right, threw right

Year Club	G.	AB.	R.	H.	2B.	3B.	HR.	RBI.	SB.	B.A.
1946–Nashua	113	396	75	115	19	8	13	96	16	.290
1947–Montreal	135	440	64	120	25	3	13	75	7	.273
1948–St. Paul	35	123	31	40	5	2	13	39	0	.325
1948–Brooklyn	83	279	32	72	11	3	9	45	3	.258
1949–Brooklyn	130	436	65	125	22	2	22	82	3	.287
1950–Brooklyn	126	437	70	123	19	3	31	89	1	.281
1951–Brooklyn	143	505	90	164	33	1	33	108	1	.325
1952–Brooklyn	128	468	73	126	18	1	22	97	8	.269
1953–Brooklyn	144	519	103	162	26	3	41	142	4	.312
1954–Brooklyn	111	397	43	82	14	3	19	51	1	.207
1955–Brooklyn	123	446	81	142	20	1	32	107	2	.318
1956–Brooklyn	124	388	39	85	6	1	20	73	1	.219
1957–Brooklyn	103	330	31	80	9	0	13	62	1	.242
Major League Totals	1215	4205	627	1161	178	18	242	856	25	.276

WORLD SERIES RECORD

Year Club	G.	AB.	R.	H.	2B.	3B.	HR.	RBI.	SB.	B.A.
1949–Brooklyn	5	15	2	4	1	0	1	2	0	.267
1952–Brooklyn	7	28	0	6	0	0	0	1	0	.214
1953–Brooklyn	6	22	6	6	0	0	1	2	0	.273
1955–Brooklyn	7	27	4	7	3	0	2	4	0	.259
1956–Brooklyn	7	22	2	4	1	0	0	3	0	.182
World Series Totals	32	114	14	27	5	0	4	12	0	.237

Voted Most Valuable Player 1951, 1953, 1955.

GORDON STANLEY "MICKEY" COCHRANE

Year	Club	League	G.	AB.	R.	H.	2B.	3B.	HR.	RBI.	B.A.	PO.	A.	E.	F.A.
1923–Dover		East. Sh.	65	245	56	79	12	6	5	....	.322	222	70	13	.957
1924–Portland		P. C.	99	300	43	100	8	5	7	56	.333	278	49	14	.959
1925–Philadelphia		Amer.	134	420	69	139	21	5	6	55	.331	419	79	8	.984
1926–Philadelphia		Amer.	120	370	50	101	8	9	8	47	.273	502	90	15	.975
1927–Philadelphia		Amer.	126	432	80	146	20	6	12	80	.338	559	85	9	.986
1928–Philadelphia		Amer.	131	468	92	137	26	12	10	57	.293	645	71	25	.966
1929–Philadelphia		Amer.	135	514	113	170	37	8	7	95	.331	659	77	13	.983
1930–Philadelphia		Amer.	130	487	110	174	42	5	10	85	.357	654	69	5	.993
1931–Philadelphia		Amer.	122	459	87	160	31	6	17	89	.349	560	63	9	.986
1932–Philadelphia		Amer.	139	518	118	152	35	4	23	112	.293	652	94	5	.993
1933–Philadelphia		Amer.	130	429	104	138	30	4	15	60	.322	476	67	6	.989
1934–Detroit		Amer.	129	437	74	140	32	1	2	76	.320	517	69	7	.988
1935–Detroit		Amer.	115	411	93	131	33	3	5	47	.319	504	50	6	.989
1936–Detroit		Amer.	44	126	24	34	8	0	2	17	.270	159	13	3	.983
1937–Detroit		Amer.	27	98	37	30	10	1	2	12	.306	103	13	0	1.000
Major League Totals			1482	5169	1041	1652	333	64	119	832	.320	6409	840	111	.985

WORLD'S SERIES RECORD

Year	Club	League	G.	AB.	R.	H.	2B.	3B.	HR.	RBI.	B.A.	PO.	A.	E.	F.A.
1929–Philadelphia		Amer.	5	15	5	6	1	0	0	0	.400	59	2	0	1.000
1930–Philadelphia		Amer.	6	18	5	4	1	0	2	4	.222	39	1	1	.976
1931–Philadelphia		Amer.	7	25	2	4	0	0	0	1	.160	40	4	1	.978
1934–Detroit		Amer.	7	28	2	6	1	0	0	1	.214	36	5	0	1.000
1935–Detroit		Amer.	6	24	3	7	1	0	0	1	.292	32	3	1	.972
World's Series Totals			31	110	17	27	4	0	2	7	.245	206	15	3	.987

WILLIAM MALCOLM DICKEY

Year Club	League	G.	AB.	R.	H.	2B.	3B.	HR.	RBI.	B.A.	PO.	A.	E.	F.A.
1925—Little Rock	South.	3	10	1	3	0	0	0	...	.300	8	2	0	1.000
1926—Muskogee	W. A.	61	212	27	60	6	2	7	...	.283	300	58	13	.965
1926—Little Rock	South.	21	46	6	18	1	5	0	8	.391	36	4	2	.952
1927—Jackson	Cot. St.	101	364	46	108	31	3	3	...	.297	457	84	9	.984
1928—Little Rock	South.	60	203	22	61	12	6	4	32	.300	151	52	8	.962
1928—Buffalo	Int.	3	8	0	1	0	1	0	0	.125	12	4	2	.889
1928—New York	Amer.	10	15	1	3	1	1	0	2	.200	7	2	0	1.000
1929—New York	Amer.	130	447	60	145	30	6	10	65	.324	476	95	12	.979
1930—New York	Amer.	109	366	55	124	25	7	5	65	.339	318	51	11	.971
1931—New York	Amer.	130	477	65	156	17	10	6	78	.327	670	78	3	.996
1932—New York	Amer.	108	423	66	131	20	4	15	84	.310	639	53	9	.987
1933—New York	Amer.	130	478	58	152	24	8	14	97	.318	721	82	6	.993
1934—New York	Amer.	104	395	56	127	24	4	12	72	.322	527	49	8	.986
1935—New York	Amer.	120	448	54	125	26	6	14	81	.279	536	62	3	.995
1936—New York	Amer.	112	423	99	153	26	8	22	107	.362	499	61	14	.976
1937—New York	Amer.	140	530	87	176	35	2	29	133	.332	692	80	7	.991
1938—New York	Amer.	132	454	84	142	27	4	27	115	.313	518	74	8	.987
1939—New York	Amer.	128	480	98	145	23	3	24	105	.302	571	57	7	.989
1940—New York	Amer.	106	372	45	92	11	1	9	54	.247	425	55	3	.994
1941—New York	Amer.	109	348	35	99	15	5	7	71	.284	422	45	3	.994
1942—New York	Amer.	82	268	28	79	13	1	2	37	.295	322	44	9	.976
1943—New York	Amer.	85	242	29	85	18	2	4	33	.351	322	37	2	.994
1944-45—New York	Amer.	(In Military Service)												
1946—New York	Amer.	54	134	10	35	8	0	2	10	.261	201	29	3	.987
1947—Little Rock	South.	8	12	2	4	2	0	1	2	.333	12	2	0	1.000
Major League Totals		1789	6300	930	1969	343	72	202	1209	.313	7866	954	108	.988

WORLD'S SERIES RECORD

Year Club	League	G.	AB.	R.	H.	2B.	3B.	HR.	RBI.	B.A.	PO.	A.	E.	F.A.
1932—New York	Amer.	4	16	2	7	0	0	0	4	.438	25	1	0	1.000
1936—New York	Amer.	6	25	5	3	0	0	1	5	.120	38	4	1	.977
1937—New York	Amer.	5	19	3	4	0	1	0	3	.211	26	1	0	1.000
1938—New York	Amer.	4	15	2	6	0	0	1	2	.400	31	5	0	1.000
1939—New York	Amer.	4	15	2	4	0	0	2	5	.267	27	2	0	1.000
1941—New York	Amer.	5	18	3	3	1	0	0	1	.167	24	2	0	1.000
1942—New York	Amer.	5	19	1	5	0	0	0	0	.263	25	1	1	.963
1943—New York	Amer.	5	18	1	5	0	0	1	4	.278	28	3	0	1.000
World's Series Totals		38	145	19	37	1	1	5	24	.255	224	19	2	.992

CHARLES LEO "GABBY" HARTNETT

Year	Club	League	Pos.	G.	AB.	R.	H.	2B.	3B.	HR.	RBI.	B.A.	PO.	A.	E.	F.A.
1921—Worcester	East.		C	100	345	38	91	21	7	3	...	.264	447	104	19	.967
1922—Chicago	Nat.		C	31	72	4	14	1	1	0	4	.194	79	29	2	.982
1923—Chicago	Nat.		C-1B	85	231	28	62	12	2	8	39	.268	413	39	5	.989
1924—Chicago	Nat.		C	111	354	56	106	17	7	16	67	.299	369	97	18	.963
1925—Chicago	Nat.		C	117	398	61	115	28	3	24	67	.289	409	114	23	.958
1926—Chicago	Nat.		C	93	284	35	78	25	3	8	41	.275	307	86	9	.978
1927—Chicago	Nat.		C	127	449	56	132	32	5	10	80	.294	479	99	16	.973
1928—Chicago	Nat.		C	120	388	61	117	26	9	14	57	.302	455	103	6	.989
1929—Chicago	Nat.		C	25	22	2	6	2	1	1	9	.273	4	0	0	1.000
1930—Chicago	Nat.		C	141	508	84	172	31	3	37	122	.339	646	68	8	.989
1931—Chicago	Nat.		C	116	380	53	107	32	1	8	70	.282	444	68	10	.981
1932—Chicago	Nat.		C	121	406	52	110	25	3	12	52	.271	484	75	10	.982
1933—Chicago	Nat.		C	140	490	55	135	21	4	16	88	.276	550	77	7	.989
1934—Chicago	Nat.		C	130	438	58	131	21	1	22	90	.299	605	86	3	.996
1935—Chicago	Nat.		C	116	413	67	142	32	6	13	91	.344	477	77	9	.984
1936—Chicago	Nat.		C	121	424	49	130	25	6	7	64	.307	504	75	5	.991
1937—Chicago	Nat.		C	110	356	47	126	21	6	12	82	.354	436	65	2	.996
1938—Chicago	Nat.		C	88	299	40	82	19	1	10	59	.274	358	40	2	.995
1939—Chicago	Nat.		C	97	306	36	85	18	2	12	59	.278	336	47	3	.992
1940—Chicago	Nat.		C	37	64	3	17	3	0	1	12	.266	69	9	4	.951
1941—New York	Nat.		C	64	150	20	45	5	0	5	26	.300	138	15	1	.994
1942—Indianapolis	A.A.		C	72	186	17	41	12	2	4	24	.220	190	36	7	.970
1943—Jersey City	Int.		C	16	16	0	4	1	0	0	5	.250	9	4	1	.929
1944—Jersey City	Int.		C-PH	13	11	1	2	1	0	0	6	.182	0	0	0	.000
Major League Totals				1990	6432	867	1912	396	64	236	1179	.297	7562	1269	143	.984

184

WORLD SERIES RECORD

Year Club	League	Pos.	G.	AB.	R.	H.	2B.	3B.	HR.	RBI.	B.A.	PO.	A.	E.	F.A.
1929—Chicago	Nat.	PH	3	3	0	0	0	0	0	0	.000	0	0	0	.000
1932—Chicago	Nat.	C	4	16	2	5	0	0	1	1	.313	31	5	1	.973
1935—Chicago	Nat.	C	6	24	1	7	0	0	1	2	.292	33	6	0	1.000
1938—Chicago	Nat.	C	3	11	0	1	0	1	0	0	.091	14	3	0	1.000
World Series Totals			16	54	3	13	2	1	2	3	.241	78	14	1	.989

ALL-STAR GAME RECORD

Year League	Pos.	AB.	R.	H.	2B.	3B.	HR.	RBI.	B.A.	PO.	A.	E.	F.A.
1933—National	C	1	0	0	0	0	0	0	.000	2	0	0	1.000
1934—National	C	2	0	0	0	0	0	0	.000	9	0	0	1.000
1935—National	C	0	0	0	0	0	0	0	.000	3	0	0	1.000
1936—National	C	4	1	1	0	1	0	1	.250	7	0	0	1.000
1937—National	C	3	1	1	0	0	0	0	.333	6	0	0	1.000
All-Star Game Totals		10	2	2	0	1	0	1	.200	27	0	0	1.000

RECORD AS MANAGER

Year Club	League	Pos.	W.	L.
1938—Chicago	Nat.	First	44	27
1939—Chicago	Nat.	Fourth	84	70
1940—Chicago	Nat.	Fifth	75	79
1942—Indianapolis	A.A.	Sixth	76	78

Year Club	League	Pos.	W.	L.
1943—Jersey City	Int.	Eighth	60	93
1944—Jersey City	Int.	Fifth	74	79
1945—Jersey City	Int.	Fifth	71	82
1946—Buffalo	Int.	Fifth	78	75

185

ELSTON GENE HOWARD

Year	Club	League	Pos.	G.	AB.	R.	H.	2B.	3B.	HR.	RBI.	B.A.	PO.	A.	E.	F.A.
1950—Muskegon	....	Cent.	OF	54	184	22	52	6	2	9	42	.283	61	8	3	.958
1951-52—Binghamton		East.							(In Military Service)							
1953—Kansas City	..	A.A.	OF-C	139	497	58	142	22	9	10	70	.286	228	20	10	.963
1954—Toronto	.....	Int.	C-OF	138	497	78	164	21	16	22	109	.330	588	42	8	.985
1955—New York	....	Amer.	OF-C	97	279	33	81	8	7	10	43	.290	147	13	3	.987
1956—New York	....	Amer.	OF-C	98	290	35	76	8	3	5	34	.262	205	16	1	.976
1957—New York	....	Am.	O-C-1B	110	356	33	90	13	4	8	44	.253	266	19	6	.975
1958—New York	....	Am.	C-O-1B	103	376	45	118	19	5	11	66	.314	447	29	2	.996
1959—New York	..	Am.	1B-C-O	125	443	59	121	24	6	18	73	.273	712	49	10	.987
1960—New York	....	Amer.	C-OF	107	323	29	79	11	3	6	39	.245	410	40	6	.987
1961—New York	....	Amer.	C-1B	129	446	64	155	17	5	21	77	.348	725	47	6	.992
1962—New York	....	Amer.	C	136	494	63	138	23	5	21	91	.279	713	44	4	.995
1963—New York	....	Amer.	C	135	487	75	140	21	6	28	85	.287	786	51	5	.994
1964—New York	....	Amer.	C	150	550	63	172	27	3	15	84	.313	939	67	2	.998
1965—New York	....	Amer.	C-1-O	110	391	38	91	15	1	9	45	.233	644	44	6	.991
1966—New York	....	Amer.	C-1B	126	410	38	105	19	2	6	35	.256	665	52	9	.988
1967—N.Y.-Boston	..	Amer.	C-1B	108	315	22	56	9	0	4	28	.178	536	40	6	.990
Major League Totals	....			1534	5160	597	1422	214	50	162	744	.276	7195	511	66	.992

WORLD SERIES RECORD

Year	Club	League	Pos.	G.	AB.	R.	H.	2B.	3B.	HR.	RBI.	B.A.	PO.	A.	E.	F.A.
1955—New York		Amer.	OF	7	26	3	5	0	0	1	3	.192	11	1	0	1.000
1956—New York		Amer.	OF	1	5	1	2	1	0	1	1	.400	2	0	0	1.000
1957—New York		Amer.	1B	6	11	2	3	0	0	1	3	.273	22	1	1	.958
1958—New York		Amer.	OF	6	18	4	4	0	0	0	2	.222	14	2	0	1.000
1960—New York		Amer.	C-PH	5	13	4	6	1	1	1	4	.462	11	0	0	1.000
1961—New York		Amer.	C	5	20	5	5	3	0	1	1	.250	31	1	0	1.000
1962—New York		Amer.	C	6	21	1	3	1	0	0	1	.143	37	2	0	1.000
1963—New York		Amer.	C	4	15	0	5	0	0	0	1	.333	30	2	0	1.000
1964—New York		Amer.	C	7	24	5	7	1	0	0	2	.292	40	1	1	.977
1967—Boston		Amer.	C	7	18	0	2	0	0	0	1	.111	23	1	0	1.000
World Series Totals				54	171	25	42	7	1	5	19	.246	221	10	2	.991

ALL-STAR GAME RECORD

Year	League	Pos.	AB.	R.	H.	2B.	3B.	HR.	RBI.	B.A.	PO.	A.	E.	F.A.
1960—American (first game)		C	1	0	0	0	0	0	0	.000	4	0	0	1.000
1961—American (both games)		C	2	0	0	0	0	0	0	.000	6	0	0	1.000
1962—American (second game)		C	2	0	0	0	0	0	0	.000	2	0	0	1.000
1963—American		C	1	0	0	0	0	0	0	.000	5	0	0	1.000
1964—American		C	3	1	0	0	0	0	0	.000	9	0	0	1.000
All-Star Game Totals			9	1	0	0	0	0	0	.000	26	0	0	1.000

JOSEPH PAUL TORRE

Year	Club	League	Pos.	G.	AB.	R.	H.	2B.	3B.	HR.	RBI.	B.A.	PO.	A.	E.	F.A.
1960—Eau Claire	.. North.		C	117	369	63	127	23	3	16	74	.344	636	64	9	.987
1960—Milwaukee	...Nat.		PH	2	2	0	1	0	0	0	0	.500	0	0	0	.000
1961—Louisville	...A.A.		C	27	111	18	38	8	2	3	24	.342	185	14	2	.990
1961—Milwaukee	...Nat.		C	113	406	40	113	21	4	10	42	.278	494	50	10	.982
1962—Milwaukee	...Nat.		C	80	220	23	62	8	1	5	26	.282	325	39	5	.986
1963—Milwaukee	...Nat.		C-1B-OF	142	501	57	147	19	4	14	71	.293	919	76	6	.994
1964—Milwaukee	...Nat.		C-1B	154	601	87	193	36	5	20	109	.321	1081	94	7	.994
1965—Milwaukee	...Nat.		C-1B	148	523	68	152	21	1	27	80	.291	1022	73	8	.993
1966—Atlanta	......Nat.		C-1B	148	546	83	172	20	3	36	101	.315	873	87	12	.988
1967—Atlanta	......Nat.		C-1B	135	477	67	132	18	1	20	68	.277	785	81	8	.991
Major League Totals				922	3276	425	972	143	19	132	497	.297	5499	500	56	.991

ALL-STAR GAME RECORD

Year	League	Pos.	AB.	R.	H.	2B.	3B.	HR.	RBI.	B.A.	PO.	A.	E.	F.A.
1964—National		C	2	0	0	0	0	0	0	.000	5	0	0	1.000
1965—National		C	4	1	1	0	0	1	2	.250	5	1	0	1.000
1966—National		C	3	0	0	0	0	0	0	.000	5	0	0	1.000
1967—National		C	2	0	0	0	0	0	0	.000	4	1	0	1.000
All-Star Game Totals			11	1	1	0	0	1	2	.091	19	2	0	1.000

ROGER PHILLIP "DUKE" BRESNAHAN

Year—Club	League	G.	AB.	R.	H.	2B.	3B.	HR.	SB.	B.A.	PO.	A.	E.	F.A.
1897—Washington	Nat.	7	18	2	6	0	0	0	0	.333	2	8	0	1.000
1898—Toledo	Int. State	4	12	0	5	3	0	0	0	.417	1	3	1	.800
1899—Minneapolis	Western	3	1	0	1	0	1	0	0	1.000	1	5	1	.857
1900—Chicago	Nat.	1	2	0	0	0	0	0	0	.000	0	0	0	.000
1901—Baltimore	Amer.	86	293	40	77	9	9	1	10	.263	193	69	20	.929
1902—Baltimore	Amer.	66	234	31	64	9	6	4	11	.274	141	72	20	.914
1902—New York	Nat.	50	178	16	52	8	3	1	6	.292	113	25	8	.945
1903—New York	Nat.	111	406	87	142	30	8	4	34	.350	150	14	6	.965
1904—New York	Nat.	107	402	81	114	21	8	5	13	.284	151	14	8	.954
1905—New York	Nat.	95	331	58	100	18	3	0	11	.302	492	114	19	.970
1906—New York	Nat.	124	405	69	114	22	4	0	25	.281	478	131	17	.973
1907—New York	Nat.	104	328	57	83	9	7	4	15	.253	483	94	8	.986
1908—New York	Nat.	139	449	70	127	25	3	1	14	.283	657	140	12	.985
1909—St. Louis	Nat.	69	234	27	57	4	1	0	11	.244	211	78	12	.960
1910—St. Louis	Nat.	78	234	35	65	15	3	0	13	.278	295	100	16	.961
1911—St. Louis	Nat.	78	227	22	63	17	8	3	4	.278	325	102	14	.968
1912—St. Louis	Nat.	48	108	8	36	7	2	1	4	.333	138	49	5	.974
1913—Chicago	Nat.	69	162	20	37	5	2	1	7	.228	194	67	10	.963
1914—Chicago	Nat.	101	248	42	69	10	4	0	14	.278	365	113	11	.978
1915—Chicago	Nat.	77	221	19	45	8	1	1	19	.204	345	95	8	.982
1916—Toledo	A.A.	44	120	19	29	6	1	2	4	.242	95	13	0	1.000
1917—Toledo	A.A.	40	80	10	22	5	0	0	1	.275	67	20	3	.967
1918—Toledo	A.A.	19	52	4	12	2	0	1	0	.231	24	1	1	.962
National League Totals		1258	3953	613	1110	199	57	21	190	.281	4399	1144	154	.973
American League Totals		152	527	71	141	18	15	5	21	.268	334	141	40	.922
Major League Totals		1410	4480	684	1251	217	72	26	211	.279	4733	1285	194	.969

WORLD'S SERIES RECORD

Year—Club	League	G.	AB.	R.	H.	2B.	3B.	HR.	RBI.	B.A.	PO.	A.	E.	F.A.
1905—New York	Nat.	5	16	3	5	2	0	0	1	.313	27	7	0	1.000

189

JOHN KLING

Year Club	League	G.	AB.	R.	H.	2B.	3B.	HR.	SB.	B.A.	PO.	A.	E.	F.A.
1896—Houston	Texas	51	202	47	72	7	5	3	18	.356				.951
1900—St. Joseph	Western	108	442	75	133				23	.301	441	107	28	.923
1900—Chicago	Nat.	15	51	8	15	3	1	0	0	.294	48	12	5	.953
1901—Chicago	Nat.	70	253	25	67	5	3	0	7	.265	338	70	20	.977
1902—Chicago	Nat.	113	434	50	124	15	6	0	23	.286	477	160	15	.969
1903—Chicago	Nat.	132	491	67	146	29	13	3	23	.297	565	189	24	.974
1904—Chicago	Nat.	120	452	41	110	18	0	2	7	.348	499	135	17	.966
1905—Chicago	Nat.	110	380	26	83	8	6	1	13	.218	538	136	24	.982
1906—Chicago	Nat.	99	343	45	107	15	8	2	14	.312	520	126	12	.987
1907—Chicago	Nat.	100	334	44	95	15	8	1	9	.284	499	149	16	.979
1908—Chicago	Nat.	125	424	51	117	23	5	4	16	.276	596			
1909—							Out of game							
1910—Chicago	Nat.	86	297	31	80	17	2	2	3	.269	407	118	11	.979
1911—Chi.-Bos.	Nat.	97	321	40	68	11	3	3	1	.212	424	140	26	.956
1912—Boston	Nat.	81	252	26	80	10	3	2	3	.317	322	108	19	.958
1913—Cincinnati	Nat.	80	209	20	57	7	6	0	2	.273	259	94	9	.975
Major League Totals		1228	4241	474	1149	176	64	20	121	.271	5492	1546	206	.972

WORLD'S SERIES RECORD

Year Club	League	G.	AB.	R.	H.	2B.	3B.	HR.	SB.	B.A.	PO.	A.	E.	F.A.
1906—Chicago	Nat.	6	17	2	3	0	0	0	0	.176	37	10	1	.979
1907—Chicago	Nat.	5	19	2	4	1	0	0	0	.211	25	9	1	.971
1908—Chicago	Nat.	5	16	2	4	1	0	0	0	.250	32	6	0	1.000
1910—Chicago	Nat.	5	13	0	1	0	0	0	0	.077	11	7	0	1.000
World's Series Totals		21	65	6	12	2	0	0	0	.185	105	32	2	.986

ERNEST JOHNNY LOMBARDI

Year	Club	League	G.	AB.	R.	H.	2B.	3B.	HR.	RBI.	B.A.	PO.	A.	E.	F.A.
1926—Oakland		P. C.	4	6		2	1	0	0		.333	8	0	0	1.000
1927—Oakland		P. C.	16	20	2	3	0	0	1	6	.150	12	4	0	1.000
1927—Ogden		Utah-Id.	50	186	29	74	16	1	4		.398	183	40	9	.961
1928—Oakland		P. C.	120	318	39	120	27	3	8	47	.377	257	47	15	.953
1929—Oakland		P. C.	164	516	70	189	36	3	24	109	.366	521	95	16	.975
1930—Oakland		P. C.	146	473	76	175	32	4	22	105	.370	563	105	17	.975
1931—Brooklyn		Nat.	73	182	20	54	7	1	4	23	.297	218	23	4	.984
1932—Cincinnati		Nat.	118	413	43	125	22	9	11	68	.303	288	76	14	.963
1933—Cincinnati		Nat.	107	350	30	99	21	1	4	47	.283	223	52	8	.972
1934—Cincinnati		Nat.	132	417	42	127	19	4	9	62	.305	383	61	5	.989
1935—Cincinnati		Nat.	120	332	36	114	23	3	12	64	.343	298	49	6	.983
1936—Cincinnati		Nat.	121	387	42	129	23	2	12	68	.333	330	54	15	.962
1937—Cincinnati		Nat.	120	368	41	123	22	1	9	59	.334	333	58	11	.973
1938—Cincinnati		Nat.	129	489	60	167	30	1	19	95	.342	512	73	9	.985
1939—Cincinnati		Nat.	130	450	43	129	26	2	20	85	.287	536	63	10	.984
1940—Cincinnati		Nat.	109	376	50	120	22	0	14	74	.319	397	46	5	.989
1941—Cincinnati		Nat.	117	398	33	105	12	1	10	60	.264	496	70	10	.983
1942—Boston		Nat.	105	309	32	102	14	0	11	46	.330	251	41	6	.980
1943—New York		Nat.	104	295	19	90	7	0	10	51	.305	296	36	10	.971
1944—New York		Nat.	117	373	37	95	13	0	10	58	.255	350	47	13	.968
1945—New York		Nat.	115	368	46	113	7	1	19	70	.307	425	49	8	.983
1946—New York		Nat.	88	238	19	69	4	1	12	39	.290	272	36	7	.978
1947—New York		Nat.	48	110	8	31	5	0	4	21	.282	86	11	2	.980
1948—Sacramento-Oak.		P. C.	102	284	25	75	13	0	11	55	.264	267	37	8	.974
Major League Totals			1853	5855	601	1792	277	27	190	990	.306	5694	845	143	.979

WORLD'S SERIES RECORD

Year	Club	League	G.	AB.	R.	H.	2B.	3B.	HR.	RBI.	B.A.	PO.	A.	E.	F.A.
1939—Cincinnati		Nat.	4	14	0	3	0	0	0	2	.214	22	1	1	.958
1940—Cincinnati		Nat.	2	3	0	1	1	0	0	0	.333	4	0	0	1.000
World's Series Totals			6	17	0	4	1	0	0	2	.235	26	1	1	.964

191

About the Author

MILTON J. SHAPIRO was born in Brooklyn, New York, and attended P.S. 115 and Boys High School there. At college (C.C.N.Y.) he majored in advertising and public relations and was editor of *Ticker,* the undergraduate newspaper. While a senior, he got a job as a copy boy on a New York newspaper and six months later moved up to the Sports Department, where he covered all the major sports, particularly baseball. In his spare time he started writing sports biographies, and has become one of the most popular writers in that field. He is associated with a number of national magazines and finds time, in between, for books on a variety of sports subjects.